The Federation of
Asian Bishops'
Conferences
(FABC)

The Federation of Asian Bishops' Conferences (FABC)

Bearing Witness to the Gospel and the Reign of God in Asia

Jonathan Y. Tan

FORTRESS PRESS
MINNEAPOLIS

THE FEDERATION OF ASIAN BISHOPS' CONFERENCES (FABC)
Bearing Witness to the Gospel and the Reign of God in Asia

Cover design by Alisha Lofgren

Print ISBN: 978-1-5064-3355-4
eBook ISBN: 978-1-5064-3356-1

To

Peter C. Phan, PhD, STD, DD

William Cenkner, OP, PhD

David N. Power, OMI, STD

John Baldovin, SJ, PhD

Mary E. McGann, RSCJ, PhD

Louis Weil, STD

Kenan Osborne, OFM, DTheol

*doctissimis theologis in
profunda gratitudine*

Contents

Preface

Anniversaries and milestones are often good opportunities to review how far we have come, to take stock of the successes and shortcomings, and to look forward to the possibilities and opportunities ahead. The year 2022 marks an important anniversary in the history of the Asian Catholic Church and contemporary Asian Catholic theology. Fifty years ago, in 1972, the Federation of Asian Bishops' Conferences (FABC) was formally constituted by the Vatican, following the decision of the Asian Bishops' Meeting (ABM) on November 29, 1970, in Manila to establish an umbrella organization for mutual collaboration and cooperation.

On the one hand, the FABC is not as well known globally as its Latin American counterpart, the Consejo Episcopal Latinoamericano, or Latin American Episcopal Conference, better known by its acronym CELAM. It was CELAM's second conference, the celebrated 1968 Medellín Conference in Colombia, that placed Latin American theologizing on the global map when it endorsed the then emerging liberation theology and promoted the new ecclesial paradigm of *comunidades eclesiales de base* (basic ecclesial communities, or base communities). Since then, the latter part of the twentieth century has witnessed the widespread acceptance and adoption of Latin American liberation theology across Europe, North America, Africa, and Asia.

On the other hand, while it is true that the FABC is not typically on the radar of many European and North American theologians and church leaders, behind the scenes, the FABC has been articulating a new way of being church, doing theology, and bearing witness to Jesus and the Reign of God in the intercultural and plurireligious societies across postcolonial Asia. Its many statements and documents speak of the need to listen to the active presence and saving power of God's Spirit at work in the multitudes of Asia so as to be able to witness the salvific message of Jesus and the presence of God's Reign amid the diverse cultures, religions, and marginalizing life experiences across postcolonial Asia. In doing so, the FABC has laid the groundwork for an intersectional approach to doing theology in postcolonial Asia that seeks to integrate intercultural, interreligious, and liberative dimensions of theologizing in its much-heralded threefold theology of dialogue with the subaltern masses of Asia in the fullness of their diverse cultures, many religions, and experiences of poverty and marginalization.

Amid the challenges of globalization, transnationalism, and the massive movements of peoples with their cultures, religions, and ways of life in this day and age, the time has come for a better understanding of the theological contributions of postcolonial Asia in general and the FABC's accomplishments in particular. In today's transnational and global world that is constantly being shaped by peoples from diverse ethnic, cultural, linguistic, and religious backgrounds who are always on the move and rubbing shoulders with each other, the task of theologizing has become more difficult and complex. These realities mean that it is no longer possible for theologians in Europe and North America to assume a static worldview and homogeneous sociocultural and religious contexts as the foundation for doing theology in Europe and North America.

Within the contemporary Christian theological tradition, the complexities of cultural diversity and religious pluralism in today's world raise the overarching question of how theological reflection can be carried out, not by excluding other cultural and religious traditions, but rather by engaging and interacting with these other religious traditions as part of the sociocultural context for theologizing in response to the question, "What is the significance and implications of understanding my neighbors' diverse cultural and faith traditions for understanding my own Christian faith tradition theologically?" As ongoing human migrations continually transform the cultural and religious landscapes of Europe and North America, how can the task of Christian theological reflection be challenged, reshaped, transformed, and enriched by engaging with these other traditions as well as the diverse forms of World Christianities that transnational migrants have brought with them to Europe and North America?

Here is where Asia comes into the picture. Although contemporary theologies emerging from Asia generally and the theological pronouncements from the FABC in particular may not be as well known globally compared to Latin American theologies and the theological pronouncements from CELAM, they are nevertheless no less important and crucial for rethinking the task of doing theology in contemporary Europe and North America. As these two places become increasingly diverse and pluralistic, Asia becomes relevant as an important source of innovative insights and new ideas for shaping the future directions of doing theology. In particular, as European and North American theologians move to reconfigure their theological worldviews, methodologies, and approaches to this new reality of immense cultural diversity and religious pluralism where Eurocentric Christianity is no longer the dominant or normative voice, they could learn a great deal from how their Asian counterparts have articulated postcolonial Asian Christian responses to this change.

As we commemorate anniversaries and milestones, I note that the year 2020 marks a personal milestone—twenty years ago, my first refereed essay on the FABC, "Theologizing at the Service of Life: The Contextual Theological Methodology of the Federation of Asian Bishops' Conferences (FABC)," appeared in the journal *Gregorianum* (Tan 2000). I remain eternally grateful to the late Fr. Jacques Dupuis, SJ, the editor of *Gregorianum*, for accepting my submission for publication. I still remember his feedback to me that this was the best systematic treatment of the FABC's contextual theology that he has read. Subsequently, I explored various aspects of the FABC's contributions to mission theology (Tan 2002, 2003a, 2003b, 2004a, 2004b, 2004c, 2005a, 2005b, 2005c, 2006b), ecclesiology (Tan 2005d, 2006a, 2013), inculturation (Tan 2001, 2011), and migration (Tan 2012).

With the benefit of hindsight afforded to me by the passage of time and space, together with feedback over the years from respondents and participants at conference panels and sessions, as well as friends and colleagues, I am able to see things in a different light, critically rethink some of my earlier ideas and points, gain new insights, and reframe my analysis and arguments in the chapters of this book. While all the chapters are new, they incorporate two decades of critical reevaluations, maturity, and wisdom. It goes without saying that it is impossible to capture the entire range and ambit of the FABC's treasure trove of theologizing. Hence it is certainly not my intent to offer an all-encompassing and comprehensive treatment of every minute aspect of the FABC's theological endeavors. Other theologians have explored themes and issues that I have not covered in this book, and I look forward to learning from what they have written about other aspects of the FABC's many contributions to the task of doing theology.

This book is divided into six chapters. The first chapter, which introduces the contemporary context of Asia, represents a complete reworking of my approach to the FABC's method to being church and doing theology in Asia. Here I have made the conscious and deliberate decision to emphasize the postcolonial dimensions of Asia and the challenges and implications of decolonization for shaping a postcolonial Asian church and way of theologizing. In doing so, I respond to a glaring lacuna in my earlier essays—the lack of a critical evaluation of the impact of decolonization and rising postcolonial consciousness for shaping a new way of being church and doing theology in contemporary Asia. The second chapter introduces the FABC and its theological approach and method. Building on chapter 1, I argue that an in-depth and critical understanding of the challenges of decolonization and the impact of postcolonialism is important to appreciate the FABC's approach to being church and doing theology in Asia. In this completely rewritten chapter from the ground up, I highlight the deeply postcolonial and intersectional dimensions of the FABC's theologizing. Here, as well as in the rest of this book, I will utilize the critical sociocultural analytical framework of *intersectionality*, which was first articulated by the Black feminist scholar Kimberlé Crenshaw (1989), to reframe the FABC's threefold dialogue with cultures, religions, and the poor as its deeply profound grasp and appreciation of the impact of the intersectional forces of cultures, religions, and subaltern experiences on being church and theologizing in postcolonial Asia.

This brings us to the third chapter, which addresses the challenges of religious pluralism for the FABC and its prophetic response—seeking to be a sacrament of unity and harmony amid much strife, violence, and conflicts. In this chapter, I also address another gap in my earlier writings by discussing for the first time the FABC's theology of care for the environment and ecology, which flows from its theology of harmony. The fourth chapter focuses on the FABC's new way of being church in postcolonial Asia, witnessing to the gospel and the Reign of God in an intersectional manner. The fifth chapter covers the FABC's maturity and coming-of-age at the 1998 Asian Synod in Rome and its aftermath, including Pope John Paul II's *Ecclesia in Asia* and the FABC's critical response. Chapter 6 discusses the new challenges and possibilities for the FABC as it looks ahead to the future. Here I explore the challenges and implications of migration, transient migration, online and virtual communities, and insider movements for shaping the future of the FABC's approach to theologizing.

I would like to express my gratitude to everyone who has assisted me in one way or another in the writing of this book. It is with deep pleasure that I express my profound thanks to my friend and colleague Dr. Jesudas Athyal—the acquiring editor in World Christianity and South Asian theology at Fortress Press and a specialist in Indian theology and scholar in South Asian religion and society in his own right—for his invitation to write this book and his gentle and constant encouragement to complete this long-overdue work. It has been difficult to find time to write this book while juggling teaching, research, service commitments, and traveling back and forth between two cities weekly. Hence it is with much relief that Case Western Reserve University granted me a much-needed sabbatical so that I could complete this book. I am also indebted to the endowment of the Archbishop Paul J. Hallinan Professorship in Catholic Studies for the funding for the research and acquisition of books and other reading materials for this book. I am especially indebted to the late Fr. Edward Malone, MM, the deputy secretary-general of the FABC, and Fr. James Kroeger, MM, at Loyola School of Theology in Manila, for their help in obtaining all the FABC documentation and resources. This book could not have been written without their assistance.

This book also benefited from the valuable feedback of the participants at several conferences where I presented early draft versions of selected chapters as conference papers. Their questions, comments, and critiques helped me clarify what I meant to say, as well as rethink and refine those tentative arguments that were previously ambiguous or shaky. I presented excerpts from the first chapter as a plenary paper at the Ninth International Gathering of the Ecclesiological Investigations International Research Network at Georgetown University in May 2015. Portions of chapters 2, 3, and 4 were presented as a plenary paper documenting the FABC's reception of Vatican II in postcolonial Asia in the areas of ecclesiology, missiology, and interreligious dialogue. This presentation was at the International Symposium on Vatican II, *Ein Konzil der Weltkirche: hermeneutische Fragen einer internationalen Kommentierung*, which was held at the Philosophisch-theologische Hochschule Vallendar, Germany, in June 2019. An early version of chapter 6 was presented at the conference Theology without Borders: Celebrating the Legacy of Peter C. Phan at Georgetown University in March 2017.

A word of thanks to my colleagues at Case Western Reserve University as well as my colleagues and friends in Asia, Australia, and North America who have been most supportive and encouraging, including Emmanuel Nathan and Catherine Gomes in Australia; Sharon Bong and Joseph Goh in Malaysia; Christopher Soh, SJ, in Singapore; Michael Amaladoss, SJ, in India; and Gregory Hyde, SJ, Paula M. Jackson, Grace Kao, Tisha Rajendra, Orlando Espín, Jean-Pierre Ruiz, and Carmen Nanko-Fernández in the United States. My own writing has been nourished and sustained by their wise counsel, intellectual inspiration, incisive criticisms, invaluable guidance, and peer support.

My first book was dedicated to my son and his mother. My second book was dedicated to my parents. In my traditional culture, it is important to honor one's teachers for imparting their wisdom. Hence this book is dedicated to my graduate school professors at the Graduate Theological Union and the Catholic University of America with profound gratitude and deepest appreciation for their mentoring throughout the years of my graduate studies and beyond, as well as sowing the seeds for many of the ideas and insights that appear in this book.

Abbreviations

ABM	Asian Bishops' Meeting, Manila, November 29, 1970
AG	*Ad gentes, Decree on the Church's Missionary Activity*, Vatican II, December 7, 1965
AISA	Asian Institute for Social Advocacy
AsIPA	Asian Integral Pastoral Approach towards a New Way of Being Church in Asia
BILA	FABC Bishops' Institute for Lay Apostolate
BIMA	FABC Bishops' Institute for Missionary Apostolate
BIRA	FABC Bishops' Institute for Interreligious Affairs
BISA	FABC Bishops' Institute for Social Action
BISCOM	FABC Bishops' Institute for Social Communication
CBCI	Catholic Bishops' Conference of India, comprising (1) the Bishops' Synod of the Syro-Malabar Catholic Church, (2) the Holy Episcopal Synod of the Syro-Malankara Catholic Church, and (3) the Conference of Catholic Bishops of India (CCBI) of the Latin Catholic Church
CCBI	Conference of Catholic Bishops of India (Latin Catholic)

CCEO	*Codex Canonum Ecclesiarum Orientalium* (Code of Canons of the Eastern Churches)
CCM	Council of Churches of Malaysia
CCPMA	FABC Consultation on Christian Presence among Muslims in Asia
CCRM	Catholic Charismatic Renewal Movement
CELAM	Consejo Episcopal Latinoamericano (Latin American Episcopal Conference)
CFM	Christian Federation of Malaysia
CPCO	Council of Catholic Patriarchs of the East (Le Conseil des Patriarches Catholiques d'Orient)
EA	*Ecclesia in Asia*, postsynodal apostolic exhortation, Pope John Paul II, New Delhi, November 6, 1999
FABC	Federation of Asian Bishops' Conferences
FEISA	FABC Faith Encounters in Social Action
GCCRS	The Gulf Catholic Charismatic Renewal Services
GS	*Gaudium et spes, Pastoral Constitution on the Church in the Modern World*, Vatican II, December 7, 1965
ICCRS	International Catholic Charismatic Renewal Services
IMS	Indian Missionary Society
IOM	International Organization for Migration
ISAO	ICCRS Subcommittee for Asia-Oceania
LG	*Lumen gentium, Dogmatic Constitution on the Church*, Vatican II, November 21, 1964
MCCBCHST	Malaysian Consultative Council of Buddhism, Christianity, Hinduism, Sikhism, and Taoism
MLJ	*Malayan Law Journal*
NA	*Nostra aetate, Declaration on the Relation of the Church to Non-Christian Religions*, Vatican II, October 28, 1965

NECF	National Evangelical Christian Fellowship (Malaysia)
NEP	New Economic Policy (Malaysia)
PAS	Parti Islam Se-Malaysia (Pan-Malaysian Islamic Party)
RM	*Redemptoris missio, On the Permanent Validity of the Church's Missionary Mandate*, Pope John Paul II, December 7, 1990
UAE	United Arab Emirates
UCAN	Union of Catholic Asian News

1

Encountering the Postcolonial Realities of Asia

Contemporary postcolonial Asia—with around two-thirds of the world's population and its diverse array of cultures, ethnicities, languages, and spiritual and philosophical traditions, as well as social practices and ways of living—is a continent of extremes that is marked by much diversity and plurality as to defy attempts at labeling and categorization. First, the top three most populous nations in the world—namely, China, India, and Indonesia—are located in Asia. These three nations are so diverse such that they are, in reality, miniature continents with hundreds of languages and dialects, ethnic cultures, and sociocultural traditions. Second, Asia is marked by extreme diversity in languages. The Sri Lankan Jesuit theologian Aloysius Pieris explains that there are seven linguistic zones within the vast expanse of the Asian continent: Semitic, Ural-Altaic, Indo-Iranian, Dravidian, Sino-Tibetan, Malayo-Polynesian, and Japanese (1988, 70). Third, Asia is the native soil from which the ancient great religions of the world emerged, including Hinduism, Buddhism, and Jainism in South Asia; Confucianism and Daoism in East Asia; Zoroastrianism in

Central Asia; and the three monotheistic religious traditions of Judaism, Christianity, and Islam in West Asia.

While it is clear that the term *Asian* is often used as a convenient label to categorize the diverse range of peoples from the different regions of the Asian continent, in reality this term masks the significant diversity and pluralism that differentiates them in terms of worldviews, languages, ethnicities, cultures, spiritual traditions, and ways of life under the facade of a monolithic pan-Asian identity that exists more in theory than in reality. In speaking about Asia, one must bear in mind that a normative Asian culture, worldview, or way of life does not exist. As the Indian theologian Jacob Kavunkal explains succinctly,

> There is no such thing as a uniform reality of Asia.
> Asia does not have a single culture. Rather, it is a
> conglomeration of cultures and subcultures. What is
> true of a particular country in Asia need not be valid for
> other countries. Some even wonder if, apart from the
> geomorphological base which constitutes a oneness which
> can be called Asia, there is any other common defining
> element for Asia. This plurality of the Asian context is
> to be kept in mind so as to keep in sight the fact that we
> should not overlook the particularities of the individual
> Asian countries. (Kavunkal 1995, 95)

Such diversity and pluralism are evident when one takes a bird's-eye view of Asia geographically across its six principal regions. First, there is North Asia, comprising the sparsely populated Siberian region of the Russian Federation that is aligned politically, socially, and culturally with the European region of the Russian Federation, especially after the waves of resettlement of ethnic Russians there in the twentieth century. Second, West Asia—which the nineteenth-century European Orientalists labeled as "Near East" or "Middle East" and is the cradle of the monotheistic religions of Judaism, Christianity, and Islam—is a region that is predominantly Muslim today with significant pockets of Jewish and Christian presence. Ironically, Christians are fighting for their survival on their ancestral lands in West Asia, the land of Christianity's birth over two millennia ago, as they fend off ongoing sectarian conflicts and ethnoreligious violence. Third, Central Asia, through which the ancient Silk Road once ran, was historically populated by a diverse mix of Zoroastrian, Buddhist, and Assyrian Christian communities. Today, we find large communities of Muslims living in the various republics that broke away from the former Soviet Union. Fourth, South Asia, comprising the Indian subcontinent, is predominantly Hindu in India and Nepal, Buddhist in Sri Lanka, and Muslim in Pakistan and Bangladesh, with significant Muslim, Christian, Sikh, Jain, and Zoroastrian minority presence. Fifth, Southeast Asia is home to the predominantly Muslim Malay and Indonesian Archipelago on the one hand and the predominantly Buddhist Myanmar, Thailand, Vietnam, Cambodia, and Laos on the other, as well as significant diasporic and immigrant communities along ethnic, cultural, and religious lines living in their midst. Finally, East Asia—which the European Orientalists called "Far East" and encompasses China, Japan, and Korea—is heavily influenced by Confucian, Buddhist, and Daoist traditions, with a significant Muslim presence in the western regions of China that overlap into Central Asia.

What sets Asia apart from Africa, the Americas, and Oceania is the fact that European imperialism and colonial expansionism never did fully subjugate and colonize the whole of the Asian continent to the same extent as the other continents, which witnessed violent massacres and genocides of their Indigenous populace as well as the systematic destruction of their social, political, cultural, and religious fabric. As a result, much of the historical and cultural legacies of Asia as a continent with ancient civilizations, cultures, and religious traditions still endure and are very much alive today. Currently, we find in Asia the world's oldest extant civilizations of China and India on the one hand and newer nations such as Timor-Leste, which became an independent nation-state in 2002, on the other. Asia birthed several of the world's ancient civilizations, including the Mohenjo-daro, Harappa, and Dholavira civilizations in the Indus valley (ca. 3000 BCE; Agrawal 1982); the Yangshao civilization in the Yellow River basin (ca. 5000 BCE); and the Liangzhu civilization in the Yangtze River valley (ca. 3300 BCE; Chang 1986).

At the same time, contemporary Asia is a continent of extreme social, political, and economic heterogeneity ranging from autocratic dictatorships to multiparty democracies, theocracies to secular nations, communist or socialist to capitalist societies. Asia is also marked by massive socioeconomic extremes between immense wealth and deep-seated poverty, with the richest nations in West Asia that are beneficiaries of an oil boom and cheap migrant labor at the top of the economic ladder and countries such as Timor-Leste, Bangladesh, Myanmar, and Cambodia at the bottom, where the people struggle to eke out a daily living. Hence Asia is also a continent facing massive migratory movements of people from the poorer regions seeking their fortune in wealthier nations, transforming the sociocultural, religious, political, and economic landscapes across Asia. In turn, this has contributed to increasing breakdowns in the traditional social order and the loss of stable familial and communal structures, resulting in much fragmentation and tension.

Asian Christianity in the Sea of Asian Religiosities

While Asia may be the world's most populous continent, it continues to be the continent with the smallest Christian population.

According to the 2011 report *Global Christianity: A Report on the Size and Distribution of the World's Christian Population* by Pew Research Center's Forum on Religion and Public Life, Christians account for 7 percent of the total population of the Asia-Pacific region, which translates to 13.1 percent of the total global Christian population (2011, 75). *Global Christianity* further identifies the top three Asian countries with a significant Christian percentage of their total population as the Philippines (93.1 percent), Timor-Leste (99.6 percent), and South Korea (29.3 percent) and notes that Christians continue to constitute a small proportion of the residents of China (5 percent) and India (2.6 percent), who collectively make up about one-third of the world's population (75–76). It is ironic that Christians remain a minority presence in Asia, notwithstanding that Jesus was born in West Asia and Asia has had a Christian presence for more than two millennia. Indeed, the Christian movement originally emerged in Asia and also moved eastward, propagated by Assyrian Church of the East missionaries who traveled across the vast expanses of Central Asia along the Silk Road to India and China in the first Christian millennium (Gillman and Klimkeit 1999; Moffett 1998; Irvin and Sunquist 2001; Baum and Winkler 2003; Jenkins 2009).

Christianity's Minority Status in Postcolonial Asia

With the exception of the Philippines and Timor-Leste, the Christian presence across Asia is characterized by Asian Christians representing a significant minority religious community in the midst of dominant and resurgent religious majorities—for example, Islam in West, Southwest, and Central Asia and Pakistan, Indonesia, and Malaysia; Hinduism in India; and Buddhism in Sri Lanka, Myanmar, and Thailand. Although the term *minority* is controversial for its possible pejorative connotations, nonetheless it is popularly used to classify a group that is numerically small in comparison with other larger groups in its midst in terms of race, ethnicity, gender, socioeconomic class, culture, religion, or other categories. More importantly, this term almost always connotes the *imbalance* of power dynamics between a minority group vis-à-vis the dominant majority group, with the latter occupying positions of power and harassing the minority group to conform to its norms and expectations (Blalock 1967; Bonacich 1973).

The dilemma of Christianity's minority status in postcolonial Asia is further compounded by its association with European and American imperialism and colonialism in Asia. For much of the nineteenth and the first half of the twentieth century, European and American Christian missionaries and their mission societies and organizations, Protestant and Catholic, traveled across much of Asia, often in tandem with waves of European and American economic and political expansionism that were often resented by the natives. These foreign Christian missionaries had high hopes for a massive Christianization of Asia by the end of the twentieth century, displacing the great religions of the continent to become a majority religion across Asia.

For example, the Edinburgh World Missionary Conference of 1910 focused on, in the words of the American Methodist missioner John R. Mott, who presided over the conference proceedings, "the evangelization of the world in this generation." Moreover, Mott harbored the "realistic possibility" of "imminent Christian triumph" over other world religions (Stanley 2009, 15). W. Richey Hogg notes that Edinburgh 1910 reflected "the high tide of Western European optimism and imperialism" that assumed the imminent Christianization of the world was at hand (1980, 146). The church historian Stephen Neill quotes the conference delegates as confidently expecting that "as the lordship of Christ came to be recognized, these other religions would disappear in their present form—the time would come when Shiva and Vishnu would have no more worshippers than Zeus and Apollo would have today"

(1990, 418). Brian Stanley cites the opening address of Archbishop of Canterbury Randall Davidson, who was confident that "there be some standing here tonight who shall not taste of death till they see . . . the Kingdom of God come with power" (2009, 1). The Indian theologian M. Thomas Thangaraj explains, "Missionaries saw the West's colonial expansion as God's own providential way of opening the doors for preaching the gospel in the uttermost parts of the earth," while "colonizers saw missionary work as a way of subduing people in the colonies" (1999, 19).

Notwithstanding the hopeful aspirations of Edinburgh 1910 for the Christianization of the world generally and Asia in particular, the great religions have not become minorities in the midst of a Christian majority in Asia. What the delegates at Edinburgh 1910 failed to anticipate were the cataclysmic events of World War I, which erupted merely four years later in 1914, followed by the Second World War and the Shoah, undermining their claim of Christianity's moral superiority and exceptionalism over other religions. In the eyes of millions of Asians, the two world wars and the Shoah punctured the claims by colonial powers and missionaries alike of exceptional European civilization, moral-ethical superiority, and might and invincibility. No longer would these Asian masses acquiesce passively to the hegemony of the colonial powers over them and foreign missionaries preaching about the superiority of Christianity over other religions. Neill criticizes those Christian missionaries who assumed that it was business as usual after the Second World War and discounted the rising nationalist sentiments for decolonization and political independence: "And the student is again and again amazed at the Westernness of the missions. Almost everywhere it seems to be taken for granted that the missionary period will go on for ever; the duty of the convert is clear—to trust in the superior wisdom of the white man and so to be conveyed without too much trouble in the safe bark of holy Church to the everlasting kingdom in heaven" (1990,

369). The missiologist Aylward Shorter agrees with Neill when he asserts, "The old Eurocentric model of mission, in which the Western Church is credited with stability and maturity, and with the right to send missionaries to the 'pagan' nations of the non-Western world. Such new Churches are to remain indefinitely under the tutelage of the Christian West. In this paradigm, missionaries are sent by centralized organizations on behalf of the universal Church" (1994, 155).

Hence missionaries and church leaders continued to keep their colonial-era missions in Asia under their firm control, failing to devolve leadership to local Asians and creating truly local Asian churches. They could not grasp the full implications of the rising tide of decolonization, nationalism, and postcolonial consciousness, as well as the underlying tensions from these political developments that were gathering momentum throughout Asia in the ensuing decades after the end of the Second World War, which reached a high point at the 1955 Bandung Conference that birthed the Non-Aligned Movement and its unequivocal condemnation of all forms of colonialism, imperialism, domination, and hegemony over its member states (Dinkel 2019).

Moreover, Asian nations' independence from their colonial masters—independence from colonial dominance and exploitation—together with a strong sense of postcolonial consciousness resulted in the growth of national identity and pride, accompanied by a massive revival of traditional Asian religions, which have continued to grow and thrive not only in Asia but also across the world. For example, India is experiencing a Hindu renaissance, and Islam is on the upsurge across West and Southeast Asia, making it easily the fastest-growing religion in the world. In East and Southeast Asia, Buddhism has experienced a new vitality, as new Buddhist movements that first emerged in the early twentieth century have grown since the 1970s. All of these religious traditions are very much alive and influential, being intertwined within the sociocultural and political fabric across contemporary Asia, as well as nourishing the spiritual needs of billions of Asians.

Vatican II and Asian Catholics in Postcolonial Asia

When Pope John XXIII announced his intention to call an ecumenical council of more than two thousand bishops from six continents on January 25, 1959, the pontiff echoed the hopes and yearnings of many Catholics around the world, Asia included, for a new Pentecost, as well as change and renewal in a spirit of aggiornamento. The majority of the council fathers, who hailed from Europe and North America and were in charge of setting the conciliar agenda and working on the preparatory drafts of documents for consideration, had an overly hopeful and somewhat overconfident presumption that they would continue to be in control of the direction and success of reform and change around the world generally and in Asia specifically. With the benefit of hindsight, one could now see their political naivete in assuming that church growth and missionary success in Asia would continue unabated merely with tweaks and adjustments in pastoral strategies for evangelizing, inculturating, and engaging in a more positive relationship with the Asian multitudes and their vibrant religious and cultural traditions without critically considering the implications of rapid decolonization, as well as the sweeping waves of postcolonial consciousness and nationalist fervors for the church and Catholics in Asia.

Clearly, a major shortcoming of Vatican II was its failure to discuss or critique the problems of colonialism and the popular association of the missionaries with colonial empire building in any of its sixteen documents. For example, Vatican II's *Pastoral Constitution on the Church in the Modern World, Gaudium et spes,* which had much to say about developments in modernity that affected European and North American Catholics, was completely silent on the impacts and implications of colonialism on Catholics in the majority world. Instead, in Vatican II's *Decree on the Church's Missionary Activity, Ad gentes* (AG), one finds an overly confident view of the colonial status quo, with foreign missionaries remaining in charge of the missionary enterprise and the majority world Catholics as recipients of the missionary largesse. This is all the more surprising considering that the process of decolonization and former colonies seeking independence from their colonial overlords had grown over the 1950s to reach a high point by the time Vatican II met from 1962 to 1965. Hence the Filipino Jesuit theologian Felipe Gómez describes the council fathers' heady optimism concerning the future of the Catholic Church in Asia as follows:

> On Nov 6, 1964, in the 116 General Congregation of Vatican II, after Paul VI had presented the "Schema" *On the Missions*, Card. Agagianian, Prefect of *Propaganda Fide* drew a bright view of the situation: "In times of Vatican I," he said, "the Church had 275 mission territories; today, we have 770. In 1870, there was not one autonomous bishop, today we see here 41 archbishops, 126 bishops and 4 cardinals. . . . The popes had assumed the effective protagonism which they intended with the erection of the *Propaganda* in 1622 by Gregory XV. The 20th century had seen the great encyclicals *Maximum illud* (1919), *Rerum Ecclesiae* (1926), *Evangelii praecones* (1951), *Fidei donum* (1957), which channelled the missionary zeal of the secular clergy into Africa; and in the eve of the council, *Princeps pastorum* (1959)." (1986, 29)

Gómez goes on to note that "Vatican II has been accused of blindness to history, for having missed the import of decolonization, not having offered a critique of colonialism, etc. In fact, by 1965 the ancient colonies were practically all independent, only the Portuguese empire ended in 1975" (1986, 53).

In particular, the collapse of the old colonial empires had immense repercussions for Asian Catholics generally and for Catholic mission activities in Asia that were linked historically to imperial colonial enterprises through either colonial patronage—for example, the Portuguese Padroado in East Timor, Goa, Macau, and Melaka-Singapore (Boxer 1969; Teixeira 1963) or the Spanish Patronato Real in the Philippines (Costa and Schumacher 1976)—or the European colonial protectorate system, as exemplified by the French Religious Protectorate of Catholics in China and Francophone Indochina (Young 2013). In other words, the alliance of Catholic missionaries with the colonial powers during the heyday of colonial expansionism, which supported the growth of colonial Catholic missions in Asia in the face of hostilities from the local populace or persecution by native rulers, became a problematic liability in the face of rising nationalist sentiments, such that Catholic missionaries and their missions were tainted by their association and collaboration with and support from the colonial authorities. Rightly or wrongly, many Asians equated the Catholic Church's growth in Asia with colonialism's territorial expansion. The Indian Jesuit theologian Michael Amaladoss explains the dilemma as follows: "In the former colonies, Church extension is associated in the popular mind with colonialism. They certainly coincided historically and at that time the new Churches were not really built up as authentic local Churches. A certain assertion of autonomy on the part of the local Churches is not without connection to this past. Hence anything foreign is suspected and resented not only by non-Christians, but even by some Christians" (1988, 113).

Asian Christians as Religious Minorities

As a religious minority group in many parts of Asia, contemporary Asian Christians often experience complex relational dynamics with their religious majority neighbors. On the one hand, at the grassroots level, one often finds harmonious interreligious relations, as majority and minority religious groups get along in daily living without any problems—for example, Hindus, Muslims, and Christians in India making pilgrimages to each other's religious shrines and participating in communal festivals across religious boundaries (Raj and Dempsey 2002; Pechilis and Raj 2013). On the other hand, many Asian Christians have also been tarred with the same brush as the former colonial powers by nationalists and religious zealots alike, becoming a problematic liability for these Asian Christian minorities and leading to a rise in intercommunal tensions and violence against them; religion becomes politicized in response to broader socioeconomic problems.

In many parts of Asia, religious majorities are putting pressure on the Christian minorities in their midst to abandon Christianity as a colonial relic and foreign import in favor of the dominant religion of the local majority. Even religions that claim to uphold the ideals of nonviolence and tolerance—for example, Hinduism and Buddhism—have to confront the reality of prejudice, hatred, and sectarian violence by their adherents. In reality, the popular perceptions of Hindu tolerance and Buddhist pacifism have been punctured by Hindus in India and Buddhists in Sri Lanka and Myanmar who have become embroiled in violent sectarian conflicts against ethnic and religious minorities in their midst.

Not surprisingly, in many cases, interreligious conflicts against religious minorities in Asia are often linked to broader socioeconomic, political, cultural, and religious issues that are exacerbated by mass movements of people, which invariably lead to tensions between the dominant groups in the host countries and newcomer minorities. In countries such as Pakistan, India, Sri Lanka, and Myanmar, the dominant majority often resorts to the use of violence and terror to force a vulnerable minority community to conform to its definition of normative identity and belonging, resulting in communal strife and religious violence. Sadly, too often religious identities and ethnic conflicts become intertwined in sectarian violence against religious minorities, as we see in Muslims against Ahmadiyya and Christians in Pakistan, Hindus against Muslims and Christians in India, Buddhists against Hindus in Sri Lanka, and Buddhists against Muslims and Christians in Myanmar. The World Council of Churches addresses this issue in its groundbreaking document *Ecumenical Considerations for Dialogue and Relations with People of Other Religions* as follows:

> In some parts of the world, religion is increasingly identified with ethnicity, giving religious overtones to ethnic conflict. In other situations, religious identity becomes so closely related to power that the communities without power, or who are discriminated against, look to their religion as the force of mobilization of their dissent and protest. These conflicts tend to appear as, or are represented to be, conflict between religious communities, polarizing them along communal lines. Religious communities often inherit deep divisions, hatreds and enmities that are, in most cases, passed down through generations of conflict. When communities identify themselves or are identified exclusively by their religion, the situation becomes explosive, even able to tear apart communities that have lived in peace for centuries. (2004, art. 7)

India

India is an example of an Asian country where religion is caught up in a treacherous mix of caste, ethnicity, race, class, society, and politics. Notwithstanding their presence in India as an ancient religious community for almost two millennia beginning with the arrival of the Assyrian Christians who established a thriving center of Christianity along the Malabar Coast of India (Neill 1984, 42–43; Moffett 1998, 33–37), Indian Christians continue to make up only a small fraction of the total population of contemporary India. As a result, Indian Christianity has to coexist with Hinduism, Islam, Jainism, and Sikhism amid many sectarian religious rivalries. Since the 1980s, India has witnessed the strong growth of the radical groups within the militant Hindutva religious movement—such as the Vishva Hindu Parishad (VHP), Rashtriya Swayamsevak Sangh (RSS), Sangh Parivar, and Bajrang Dal—advocating Hindu pride and fomenting sectarian violence against the Muslim and Christian minorities in India as foreign and alien to Indian society, which these radical fanatics insist to be normative Hindu in culture and religion. Politically, these radical Hindutva groups are aided by the Bharatiya Janata Party (BJP) representing the political face of the Hindutva movement (Bhatt 2001). Interreligious relations between the Hindu majority and the Muslim minority fell to its lowest point with the destruction of the Babri Mosque in Ayodhya by Hindutva fundamentalists on December 6, 1992, resulting in violent clashes that left more than two thousand dead and thousands injured (Gopal 1993; Sharma 2001).

Hindu-Christian relations are just as tense and confrontational as Hindu-Muslim relations in India, with Hindutva nationalists accusing the Indian Christian minority community of proselytizing the scheduled castes and tribal communities through deceptive means in addition to using death threats to coerce Indian

Christians to abandon their faith for Hinduism (Esteves 2005). They perceive the endeavors of Indian Christians to articulate an indigenized Indian Christianity as concealing the "foreign" nature of Christianity under Indian clothing (Ghosh 2013). Since the 1990s, many Hindutva radicals have mounted vehement objections to Christian missionary outreach among the scheduled castes in Gujarat and Orissa. These objections escalated in ferocity and violence, culminating in the Australian evangelical missionary Graham Staines and his two young sons Philip and Timothy being burned alive in their station wagon in 1999. Hindutva agitators also perpetrated sectarian violence against Dalit Christians in Orissa, blaming them for the assassination of the Hindu fundamentalist Swami Lakshmanananda Saraswati, who, in reality, was assassinated by Maoist insurgents on August 24, 2008. The observations of the Indian theologian T. K. John in 1987 are especially prescient and still hold true today:

> The [Hindu] critics see Christianity as an alien and complex power structure that threatens to eventually undermine India's culture, national integrity and its religions. They feel that a religion that is disappearing from its former stronghold is being dumped, like so many unwanted drugs, on the Third World where it has to be nourished, supported and propagated by foreign money, control and power, instead of drawing its strength from the soil. They conclude that even current efforts at inculturation (which meet with so much inside opposition) are subterfuge measures to win over hesitant or unwilling recruits to the Christian fold. They accuse the Christian missionaries of taking undue advantage of the poverty, the illiteracy and ignorance of the vast majority of the people, and for the proof of this they point to the fact

that they have altogether withdrawn their "forces" from the more difficult areas like the caste Hindus, the educated and the economically well-off. (1987, 59)

In the face of the right-wing Hindutva militants perpetrating acts of vitriolic hate and sectarian violence against the Christian minority in India, the Catholic Bishops' Conference of India (CBCI) is unequivocal that one can only disarm Hindu religious exclusivism with Christian love. Hence in its response to the Orissa violence against Indian Christians, the CBCI executive committee insists that "no matter how great the threat that may confront us, we cannot renounce the heritage of love and justice that Jesus left us." This is because "when Jesus went about healing the sick, associating with outcasts and assisting the poor, those works were not allurements but the concrete realization of God's plan for humankind: to build a society founded on love, justice and social harmony" (2008, 816).

Along the same lines, the Catholic archbishop of Delhi, Vincent Concessao, explains that inflammatory Christian tracts that disparage and denigrate Hinduism are counterproductive because "they give fanatics a battering ram to crush Indian Christianity at large" (quoted in Gonsalves 2008, 806). The Indian theologian Sebastian Madathummuriyil argues the case for the Indian Catholic Church to "re-examine the Church's imperialistic objectives of mission that reflects exclusivist and totalitarian tendencies" and to rediscover its identity, "paying heed to the challenges posed by religious, cultural, ideological, and linguistic pluralism" (quoted in Boodoo 2010, 118). According to him, the Indian Catholic Church is well positioned to be a prophetic voice for peace and harmony among Hindus, Muslims, and Christians in India against the backdrop of the Hindutva ideology of homogeneity of religion, culture, and language: "To be a prophetic Church in the Indian context, then, would imply, on the one hand, forfeiting traditional strategies of mission and, on the other hand, enhancing measures for regaining trust and confidence of both Hindus and Muslims through dialogue in an age of widespread anti-Christian sentiments" (118).

Sri Lanka

Sri Lanka continues to be splintered along racial-ethnic and religious fault lines: Sinhalese against Tamil and Buddhist against Hindu and Christian. The never-ending internecine conflicts between the majority Sinhalese and minority Tamil communities have resulted in extremely toxic dynamics between these two ethnic communities. As most Sinhalese are Buddhists, while the Tamils are mainly Hindus or Christians, Sinhalese nationalists have taken to clothing their inflammatory rhetoric in the garments of Buddhist religious identity and pride (Deegalle 2006; Senanayake 2009; Grant 2009). The "Black July" anti-Tamil ethnic cleansing riots by the Sinhalese majority that erupted on July 23, 1983, led to a violent civil war between the Sinhalese majority and the Tamil minority, which finally ended in 2009 with the military defeat of the Liberation Tigers of Tamil Eelam (LTTE). During this long-running civil war, hundreds of thousands of Sri Lankan Tamils died, and many more fled as refugees. To worsen things, the use of Buddhist religious rhetoric by nationalist political parties—for example, the Jathika Hela Urumaya (National Sinhala Heritage Party)—to legitimize the civil war against the Tamil minority has poisoned peaceful inter-religious relations between the Sinhalese and the Tamils (Tambiah 1992; Hayward 2011). Established by Sinhalese Buddhist monks who entered Sri Lankan politics on a Sinhalese Buddhist nation-alist platform, the Jathika Hela Urumaya is an egregious case of religious nationalism leading to sectarian anti-Tamil violence (Bartholomeusz 2002).

On the one hand, there have been tentative efforts by the Sinhalese Buddhist majority to initiate interreligious engagements to bring about healing, reconciliation, and peace across racial-ethnic and religious boundaries. For example, the Sinhalese Buddhist activist A. T. Ariyaratne, who founded the Sarvodaya Shramadana Movement to improve the lives of villagers who experienced poverty and destruction as a result of the civil war, has sponsored peace walks and peace conferences to promote reconciliation between the Sinhalese majority and Tamil minority on the basis of shared religious values that are common to Buddhism, Hinduism, and Christianity (Ariyaratne 1999). On the other hand, similar initiatives by the Sri Lankan Christian minority have unfortunately been perceived by the Sinhalese Buddhist majority as "a sinister plan for pan-Christian domination" (Rasiah 2011, 57).

China

In China, Christians continue to be a minority community in a country that is in the midst of an impressive Buddhist, Daoist, Chinese folk religions, and Muslim revival (Wiest 2007, 531). In response to the many experts who have been predicting an explosive growth of Christianity in China (e.g., Aikman 2003; Williams 2007), Lian Xi urges caution: "Despite the phenomenal growth of Christianity in twentieth-century China, it has not come to dominate the religious scene, which is still populated primarily by Buddhist, Daoist, and syncretic folk beliefs. The underground church has in fact shown a greater tendency to absorb, and be absorbed by, popular religion than to replace it. More important, Chinese Christianity is, and will likely continue to be, primarily a religion of the masses, far from the center of policy power" (2010, 242). Commenting on the growth of Chinese Muslims, Wiest explains that the growing Chinese Muslim population in Gansu and Xinjiang is unlikely to yield up its Islamic faith to become Christian in view of the fact that the community's Islamic faith is tightly wedded to its non-Han culture and ethnic pride (2007, 531).

On a related note, Yoshiko Ashiwa and David L. Wank share Wiest's sentiments, noting that China has the world's largest Buddhist population, a thriving Daoist community, and an expanding Muslim community that is larger than the total Christian population in China (Ashiwa and Wank 2009, 1). When one looks at Buddhism in China and across East Asia, one finds a Buddhism that has gained a new vitality with new Buddhist movements that first emerged in the early twentieth century and blossomed across East Asia in the decades after the Second World War. For example, the charismatic Daisaku Ikeda has transformed the Soka Gakkai Buddhist movement from a small Japanese lay sect of Nichiren Buddhism into a global Buddhist organization with more than twelve million members in over 190 countries worldwide (Seager 2006). Established in 1967 by the Venerable Hsing Yun, the Taiwanese Buddhist dharma master, the Fo Guang Shan monastic order is the largest Chinese Mahayana Buddhist organization in the world, with temples, monasteries, schools, and universities in 173 countries across five continents. The Venerable Hsing Yun preaches an innovative practice of humanistic Buddhism that seeks to integrate Buddhist spirituality with daily ethical living, as well as to work for positive social change in this present world (Chandler 2004).

Pakistan

In many parts of Asia, relations between the Muslim majority and Christian minority are often strained and fraught with tension, especially in Pakistan, Iran, Iraq, Lebanon, and Syria, resulting in growing antagonism and hardening of attitudes toward Christian minorities living in the midst of Muslim majorities. Pakistan is an example of the troubled relations between the Christian minority and Muslim majority. From the time of the military dictatorship of the late general Muhammad Zia-ul-Haq to the present, Pakistan has witnessed an increase in attacks against the Christian minority as outsiders, including the use of the controversial blasphemy legislation to intimidate and harass Christians (Jones 2009). This led to the Roman Catholic bishop of Faisalabad, John Joseph, shooting himself in the head on May 6, 1998, in protest against the execution of a Christian on false blasphemy charges (Walbridge 2002). On August 1, 2009, Muslim zealots killed six Pakistani Christians in Gojra for allegedly desecrating the Qur'an. Pakistani Christian activists have continued to press for legal protections of the civil rights of the Pakistani Christian minority, as well as the repeal of Pakistan's all-encompassing blasphemy laws that make it very easy for Muslims to single out Christians for harassment (Jones 2009).

Malaysia

Even in a contemporary multiethnic, multilingual, multicultural, and plurireligious Asian nation like Malaysia, the Christian minority continues to experience harassment from the Muslim majority. According to the *Population Distribution and Basic Demographic Characteristic Report 2010*, 67.4 percent of citizens are Malays and other Indigenous natives, collectively classified as "Bumiputeras" by the Malaysian government, followed by 24.6 percent Chinese and 7.3 percent Indians. Around 61.3 percent of the population is Muslim. Malaysian Christians are exclusively non-Malays and hover around 9.2 percent of the population, followed by Hindus (6.3 percent) and followers of Chinese religions (1.3 percent; Malaysia Department of Statistics 2011).

Although Islam is the official religion of Malaysia and the majority of the people are Muslims, freedom of religion is guaranteed under article 11(1) of the Malaysian Federal Constitution, which states, "Every person has the right to profess and practise his religion and, subject to Clause (4), to propagate it." However, article 11(4) also empowers the federal and state governments to pass laws against the propagation of non-Muslim religions among the Muslims: "State law and in respect of the Federal Territories of Kuala Lumpur and Labuan, federal law may control or restrict the propagation of any religious doctrine or belief among persons professing the religion of Islam" (Malaysia Federal Constitution, 2010 revision).

Under the British colonial policy of divide and rule, the Malays were given political power, while control over trade and economy was given to the Chinese. This political-economic division continued postindependence, leading to much discontent among the Malays, who were envious of Chinese control of the Malaysian economy. Matters came to an explosive clash in a series of violent racial riots stoked by extremist Malay nationalists against the Chinese community beginning on May 13, 1969 (Goh 1971; Comber 1983). In the aftermath of these riots, the Malaysian government instituted the New Economic Policy (NEP) to promote national reconciliation and bridge the economic inequality between the Malays and the Chinese in an effort to rebuild a shattered civic society. Unfortunately, the NEP also institutionalized communalism, Malay dominance in nation building, and Malay sovereignty over the other minority communities in all matters political, social, and economic. This resulted in widespread economic inefficiency, corruption scandals, cronyism, and nepotism, as a small Malay elite controlled the political and economic levers of powers to the exclusion of ordinary Malays and other races (Chin 2009). As the tangible economic benefits of the NEP failed to trickle down to the ordinary Malays in rural communities, the Parti Islam Se-Malaysia (PAS), a Malaysian Islamist political party, capitalized on widespread Malay discontent to champion Islamization as the alternative to the cronyism and corruption of the NEP. In response to the popularity of PAS's Islamization platform, the ruling political elite adopted a similar policy of Islamization to blunt PAS's tactics (Kahn and Loh 1992).

Not surprisingly, the Malaysian government's heavy-handed program of Islamization has resulted in increased religious tensions between the Muslim majority vis-à-vis other religious minority communities in Malaysia. As a religious minority, Malaysian Christians have found themselves in the direct firing line of legislation and programs aimed at giving Islam a privileged position over the other religious faiths in Malaysia. For example, federal legislation was passed in 1981 to ban possession of Indonesian translations of the Bible. In response to vociferous protests by Malaysian Christians, a concession was made in 1982 to allow them to use the Indonesian translation for personal devotions and public worship. However, current law prohibits the dissemination and circulation of Indonesian and Malay translations of the Bible among Muslims in Malaysia.

Non-Muslims in Malaysia are also very upset by legislation that criminalizes apostasy (*takfir*) by Muslims and the actions of non-Muslims who proselytize their faith to Muslims in the states of Pahang, Perak, Melaka, Sabah, and Terengganu (Camilleri 2013, 231). The law against apostasy drew international headlines and condemnation in the case of Lina Joy, who filed a suit before the Malaysian Federal Court to compel the Malaysian National Registration Department to record her change of religion from Islam to Christianity on her identity card after her baptism as a Roman Catholic. On May 30, 2007, Lina Joy's appeal was dismissed by the Malaysian Federal Court in a narrow two-to-one decision in *Lina Joy v. Majlis Agama Islam Wilayah Persekutuan dan lain-lain*. In the aftermath, she and her Christian fiancé subsequently fled Malaysia under threats of violence from Muslim activists. This Malaysian Federal Court ruling further inflamed interreligious tensions, as non-Muslim minorities perceive this to be a further erosion of religious freedom in Malaysia (Walters 2007).

Another example of conflict between Malaysian Christians and Muslims is the ongoing controversy over the use of the term

Allah for God by the Christians. In 1991, the Malaysian Parliament passed legislation to prohibit this use of the term in non-Islamic literature, among other things. Malaysian Christians were outraged against this prohibition, arguing that it impinged on their right to use the term in Malay language translations of the Bible, as well as in public worship and prayer meetings (Walters 2002).

Matters came to a head in 2007, when the Malaysian minister of home affairs prohibited the Malaysian Catholic periodical *Herald Malaysia* from using the term *Allah* in its Malay-language edition. The then Catholic archbishop of Kuala Lumpur, Murphy Pakiam, sought a judicial review of the minister's decision in *Titular Roman Catholic Archbishop of Kuala Lumpur v. Menteri Dalam Negeri and Kerajaan Malaysia*. At first instance, Justice Lau Bee Lan held that the word *Allah* is not exclusive to Muslims and the minister of home affairs had no legal authority to prohibit *Herald Malaysia* from using the word in its Malay edition. Subsequently, the minister of home affairs filed an appeal against the high court's decision before the Malaysian Court of Appeal, which overturned the high court's decision in favor of the minister of home affairs in *Menteri Dalam Negeri & Ors v. Titular Roman Catholic Archbishop of Kuala Lumpur*. The archbishop of Kuala Lumpur sought leave to appeal to the federal court against the court of appeal's ruling in *Titular Roman Catholic Archbishop of Kuala Lumpur v. Menteri Dalam Negeri and Others*. On June 23, 2004, by a narrow margin of four to three, the federal court refused to grant leave to the archbishop of Kuala Lumpur, thereby affirming the court of appeal's ruling to uphold the minister of home affairs' original 2007 decision to prohibit non-Muslims from using the word *Allah* under any circumstances.

In response to the Malaysian Muslim majority's relentless pressure against Malaysian Christians, the Christian Federation of Malaysia (CFM) was established in 1986 as an umbrella organization for the Christians in Malaysia by the Roman Catholic Church, the Council of Churches of Malaysia (CCM) representing the mainline Protestant churches, and the National Evangelical Christian Fellowship (NECF) representing the Evangelical, Brethren, and Pentecostal churches. The CFM comprises about five thousand member churches and encompasses around 90 percent of the total Christian population of Malaysia. It seeks to present a united Christian front to negotiate with the Malaysian government on contentious religious issues generally and Muslim-Christian matters in particular. The CFM is also an active member of the Malaysian Consultative Council of Buddhism, Christianity, Hinduism, Sikhism, and Taoism (MCCBCHST). The MCCBCHST was established in 1983 to promote understanding, mutual respect, and co-operation among the different religions in Malaysia; resolve interreligious issues; and make representations to the Malaysian government on religious matters (Tan and Ee 1984, 13). In practice, the MCCBCHST has become an organized channel for dialogue between the non-Muslims and the Malaysian government on issues of religious freedom and the impact of encroaching Islamization on the rights of the non-Muslim religious minorities to practice their faith without interference or fear.

The fourth Catholic archbishop of Kuala Lumpur, Julian Leow, is insistent on interfaith dialogue and collaboration as the way out of the current tensions and impasse between Muslims and non-Muslims in Malaysia. In his first interview after he was chosen by Pope Francis as the new archbishop of Kuala Lumpur in 2014, he spoke of "looking forward to having inter-religious dialogues and fostering closer ties with Malaysians of various races and faiths," explaining that "once dialogue is shut out, there will be a lot of misrepresentation" (Murad 2014). In his address at his episcopal ordination, he emphasized, among other things, the need for interfaith dialogue and engagement, stating that interreligious dialogue is crucial in Malaysia to dispel misconceptions and promote mutual respect. Moreover, his commitment to interfaith engagement is also symbolically represented in his coat of arms by a "tree with religious icons," which depicts "the ability to recognize the Divine in every person we encounter [and] to be open to dialogue and to seek the good of the other" (Metropolitan Archdiocese of Kuala Lumpur, n.d.).

At the grassroots level, a number of younger Malaysians are seizing the initiative to overcome the sectarian religious divide through Projek Dialog (www.projekdialog.com). Under the leadership of two young Malaysian Muslims—cultural and political studies scholar Ahmad Fuad Rahmat and social media activist Yana Rizal—and advised by Malaysian Muslim political commentator and activist Marina Mahathir and Malaysian Lutheran Christian theologian Sivin Kit, Projek Dialog seeks to leverage social media to provide a platform for Malaysians from all religious traditions to engage in interfaith and intercultural conversations. The goal is to promote better understanding and collaboration among the diverse ethnic and religious communities in Malaysia. Projek Dialog maintains an active presence on Facebook (https://www .facebook.com/projekdialog) and Twitter (https://twitter.com/ ProjekDialog) to foster an ongoing dialogue on interfaith engagements and collaboration. To date, Projek Dialog has sponsored "interfaith walks" that seek to expose Malaysians to various religious communities and their beliefs and traditions through visits to places of worship and participation in interreligious prayer sessions and other religious activities to promote better understanding, harmony and friendship, and national unity (Pak 2013). In collaboration with the London-based human rights nongovernmental organization Article 19 (www.article19.org), Projek Dialog successfully organized a seminar titled "Freedom, Religion, and Social Media: Know Your Rights" on August 24, 2014, to explore the issues surrounding freedom of religion and human rights in the era of social media, as well as provide guidance to young Malaysian activists looking to utilize social media for advocacy on issues of religion and human rights without infringing Malaysian law generally and the Sedition Act in particular, which has been used to intimidate activists who are raising contentious issues involving religion and human rights in Malaysia.

Responding to the Experiences of the Asian Christian Minority Communities

In the various examples from different regions of Asia concerning the painful experiences of religious minority communities generally and the various Asian Christian minority communities in particular, we see firsthand how religious minority communities often experience fear, insecurity, vulnerability, and backlash from the majority for being different from the mainstream. Minorities complain about the majority scapegoating them for social ills and pressuring them to lose their distinctive racial-ethnic or religious features and become fully assimilated in the mainstream of society. Minorities come under such pressure all the time from the majority, whether it is the Christian minority in Pakistan, India, or Malaysia; the Hindu minority in Sri Lanka; and so on. This is because minority communities, unlike the majority, do not get to define the mainstream, national culture, or national identity within their societies. It is the majority who often has the political clout to enforce its values on the minorities. This is especially true in situations where the majority feels, however unwarranted the case may be, that its dominance in society, politics, and economics is under siege from the onslaught of minorities in its midst.

Hence the examples that are discussed in this chapter point to the reality that sectarian conflicts and religious strife are often caused by gross imbalances of power between majority and minority communities as well the paradox of the majority's insecurities and fears, real or unfounded, about the minority's threat to its dominance. These examples also illustrate the dangers of an "us-versus-them" rhetoric and the dominant majority's political manipulations of religious differences that go down the dangerous path of politicizing religion and playing off religious majority vis-à-vis minority communities in the interest of political expediency. The human costs of short-sighted naked power play that condones or even encourages religious violence in defense of the majority's dominant position are evident in troubled Asian nations such as Sri Lanka, Pakistan, India, Myanmar, Syria, and Iraq, where religious minorities have lost their lives or are dislocated by persecution and wars.

In the rest of this book, we will see how the Federation of Asian Bishops' Conferences (FABC) responds to the challenges that we have explored in detail in this chapter. As we unpack elements of the FABC's approach to theologizing, we will explore how it recognizes the reality that Christian minorities across Asia are often challenged to be the source of reconciliation, healing, and peace between their own communities and other communities within their societies, overcoming the majority's intolerance and extremism with acceptance and solidarity.

2

A New Way of Doing Theology in Asia

The Federation of Asian Bishops' Conferences (FABC) is a transnational body comprising fifteen Asian Catholic bishops' conferences located in East Asia, Southeast Asia, South Asia, and Central Asia as full members: Bangladesh, India, Indonesia, Japan, Kazakhstan, Korea, Laos-Cambodia, Malaysia-Singapore-Brunei, Myanmar, Pakistan, the Philippines, Sri Lanka, Taiwan, Thailand, and Vietnam. There are also ten associate members: Hong Kong, Kyrgyzstan, Macau, Mongolia, Nepal, Siberia, Tajikistan, Turkmenistan, Uzbekistan, and Timor-Leste.[1] The FABC lists its goals and objectives as follows:

1. To study ways and means of promoting the apostolate, especially in the light of Vatican II and post-conciliar official documents, and according to the needs of Asia
2. To work for and to intensify the dynamic presence of the church in the total development of the peoples of Asia
3. To help in the study of problems of common interest to the church in Asia, and to investigate possibilities of solutions and coordinated action

4. To promote inter-communication and cooperation among local churches and bishops of Asia
5. To render service to episcopal conferences of Asia in order to help them to meet better the needs of the People of God
6. To foster a more ordered development of organizations and movements in the church at the international level
7. To foster ecumenical and interreligious communication and collaboration. (Federation of Asian Bishops' Conferences [FABC] n.d.)

The impetus for the genesis of the FABC was Pope Paul VI's historic visit to the Philippines in November 1970. This papal visit marked a momentous and groundbreaking milestone in the history of Asian Catholicism. For the first time ever in the two thousand–year history of the Catholic Church, the Roman pontiff traveled beyond Europe to set foot on Asian soil. At the same time, this papal visit also provided the opportunity for the 180 Asian Catholic bishops who traveled to Manila to greet Pope Paul VI to gather in a historic meeting on November 29, 1970. The Indian theologian Felix Wilfred describes the significance of the meeting as follows: "Never before had Asian bishops come together to exchange experiences and to deliberate jointly on common questions and problems facing the continent. The meeting marked the beginning of a new consciousness of the many traditional links that united the various peoples of this region of the globe" (Wilfred 1992, xxiii). It was at this meeting that the Asian Catholic bishops agreed unanimously to the formation of a federation of various bishops' conferences to bring bishops from all corners of Asia to discuss common challenges and collaborate on mutual solutions to address these challenges, paving the way for the formal establishment of the FABC in 1972.

The FABC convenes in Plenary Assembly, its highest governing body, with the participation of all the member conferences once every four years. The Plenary Assembly comprises all the presidents of the member episcopal conferences or their official bishop designates, the bishop delegates elected by the member episcopal conferences, and members of the various standing committees. To date, eleven plenary assemblies have been held: FABC I: Evangelization in Modern Day Asia (Taipei, 1974); FABC II: Prayer—the Life of the Church in Asia (Calcutta, 1978); FABC III: The Church—a Community of Faith in Asia (Bangkok, 1982); FABC IV: The Vocation and Mission of the Laity in the Church and in the World of Asia (Tokyo, 1986); FABC V: Journeying Together toward the Third Millennium (Bandung, 1990); FABC VI: Christian Discipleship in Asia Today—Service to Life (Manila, 1995); FABC VII: A Renewed Church in Asia on a Mission of Love and Service (Samphran, Thailand, 2000); FABC VIII: The Asian Family towards a Culture of Integral Life (Daejeon, South Korea, 2004); FABC IX: Living the Eucharist in Asia (Manila, 2009); FABC X: FABC at Forty—Responding to the Challenges of Asia (Xuan Loc, Vietnam, 2012); and FABC XI: The Catholic Family in Asia—Domestic Church of the Poor on a Mission of Mercy (Colombo, Sri Lanka, 2016).

In addition to the quadrennial Plenary Assembly, there are two committees—the Central Committee, which comprises the presidents of bishops' conferences who meet every two years, and the Standing Committee, which comprises five bishops selected by the Central Committee who meet annually. Complementing the Central and Standing Committees are ten specialized offices—the offices of Human Development, Social Communication, Laity and Family, Education and Faith Formation, Ecumenical and Interreligious Affairs, Evangelization, Clergy, Consecrated Life, and Theological Concerns (formerly the FABC Theological Advisory Commission) and the Central Secretariat (Tirimanna 2014, 307). These ten offices organize and implement programs, symposia, and workshops through various bishops' institutes, including the bishops' institutes for Lay Apostolate (BILA), Missionary Apostolate

(BIMA), Interreligious Affairs (BIRA), Social Action (BISA), and Social Communication (BISCOM) and the Asian Institute for Social Advocacy (AISA). The FABC also sponsors the Faith Encounters in Social Action (FEISA) to promote interreligious dialogue through social involvement, emphasizing that the Asian church needs to ground its mission and outreach in a threefold dialogue with the Asian peoples within their cultures, religious traditions, and poverty and other life struggles.

All of these plenary statements, as well as documents and resources from the various FABC offices and their institutes, colloquia, and workshops, highlight the FABC's major accomplishments and milestones in shaping and nourishing the theological life of the Asian Catholic Church and the spiritual growth of Asian Catholics since its inception (Wilfred 1992; Bevans 1996; Fox 2002; Chia 2003). Commenting on the FABC's achievements, Felix Wilfred writes, "The FABC has created horizontal communication between the bishops and the bishops' conferences; it has fostered a spirit of collegiality, communion and cooperation among them" (1992, xxix). At the same time, Wilfred acknowledges that Asia is not a monolithic continent, and therefore, "the FABC can speak only in general terms and cannot address itself specifically to concrete situations" (xxx). The Vietnamese American theologian Peter C. Phan draws the link between Vatican II and the FABC, asserting that the FABC is "as much the most mature fruit of the process of reception" of Vatican II as well as "the most effective instrument for the implementation of the council's teaching and reform agenda" with a focus on "episcopal collegiality, ecclesial communion, and dialogue as the mode of being church, the three ecclesiological principles advocated by the council" (2018, 12).

Writing in 1996, the missiologist Stephen Bevans observed that "the FABC could look back on twenty-five years of activity which had yielded an impressive body of documents that are incredibly rich, amazingly visionary, and truly worth careful reading and study" (1996, 2). Since Bevans wrote those words in 1996, this "impressive body of documents" has multiplied to fill five volumes in a series entitled *For All the Peoples of Asia: Federation of Asian Bishops' Conferences Documents*—volume 1, 1970–91 (Rosales and Arévalo 1992); volume 2, 1992–96 (Eilers 1997); volume 3, 1997–2001 (Eilers 2002); volume 4, 2002–6 (Eilers 2007); and volume 5, 2007–12 (Tirimanna 2014). In addition, the FABC collaborates with Asian theologians through its Office of Theological Concerns, which comprises bishop and clergy theologians who collaborate closely with invited lay theologians to produce important studies, position statements, and other documents for use by the wider FABC constituencies. The fruits of these partnerships are published in a series entitled FABC Papers and are available online on its website at www.fabc.org.

On the one hand, strictly speaking, the many statements and documents of the FABC do not have juridical or canonical force. This is because under its statutes, which were approved by the Holy See in 1972, the FABC is a voluntary association of Catholic episcopal conferences in Asia with an emphasis on collaboration and partnership to contribute to the theological life of the Asian Catholic Church, as well as the pastoral care and spiritual growth in the lives of Asian Catholics. On the other hand, the Asian Catholic bishops themselves recognize that the many statements and documents of the FABC are not about canonical enforcement. Instead, they are powerful expressions of collegial solidarity that seek to empower these bishops to respond effectively to the many challenges and opportunities in their midst.

In order for us to understand and evaluate the FABC's approach to the task of doing theology in Asia, we will be examining all relevant FABC statements and documents in a synchronic manner, as well as reading them together as an integrated whole. All of them have different levels of theological authority, the most authoritative of which are the final statements of the FABC plenary assemblies, followed by the documents of the bishops' institutes and other regional or national meetings (Quatra 2000, 23–24). Miguel Marcelo Quatra explains that the documents of the FABC offices—for example, the Office of Theological Concerns—"enjoy an authority that might be called reflected, from the fact that it is an accredited instance of the Federation and of the Bishops' Conferences that chose its members" (2000, 24). Quatra further cites Domenico Colombo's observation that while the documents of the various FABC offices and bishops' institutes "do not have the same authority of the Assemblies and are an indirect expression of the FABC," they nonetheless "constitute the mechanism by which the lines of reflection and action offered to the Federation and the Assemblies are in fact drawn up and tried. In reality it is they that blaze the trail and move things forward in various directions" (Colombo 1997, 14). As Colombo explains, "The itinerary of the big Assemblies is interwoven with the activities of the Offices, without which they would remain only an ideal and abstract journey.... The texts of the various Institutes correspond to as many paths that wind through the sectors vital for the reflection and praxis of the Church in Asia. They intersect, flow into each other and receive their thrust from the plenary sessions. It is indispensable to know them in order to understand where the FABC is going and how it moves" (18; English translation taken from Quatra 2000, 24).

A Postcolonial and Intersectional Theological Approach

Looking at the extensive official statements and documents of the FABC, it should not surprise us that the FABC's approach to theologizing is one that is carried out in response to specific challenges, issues, and needs that emerge within different regions of Asia. As a keen observer, Stephen Bevans notes,

What is clearly evident as one reads the various FABC
documents is the employment of a method that starts
from experience, from lived, actual realities. In every
document issued by a plenary assembly (with the
exception of the third plenary assembly which begins with
a theology of church) and in many documents that result
from the various bishops' institutes, the starting point
for reflection is Asian reality. Asia, say the documents,
is a continent in transition, undergoing modernization,
social change and secularization. These things threaten
traditional values in Asia, and so the church needs to
witness to the rich spiritual heritage that are the hallmarks
of Asian religiosity in all its variety. (1996, 10)

Let me build on Bevans's 1996 insights by proposing that the
FABC's new way of doing theology with Asian resources may be
best explained as a postcolonial and intersectional Asian theology
that seeks to ground the salvific message of Jesus's good news
for all Asians within their lived daily experiences of diverse intercultural, multilingual, multiethnic, and plurireligious realities. In
the discussion that follows, I will seek to demonstrate how the
FABC's underlying postcolonial worldview and intersectional
understanding of Asian realities shape the manner in which the
FABC perceives and responds to the challenges to the tasks of
being church and doing theology in the midst of cultural diversity,
religious plurality, and subaltern experiences across Asia.

A Postcolonial Theology

For much of the past two millennia of Christian history, classical
European theologies have emphasized the two *loci theologici* of
Scripture and tradition as normative and universal for the task
of theologizing regardless of context or location. In turn, such a

normative and overarching understanding of European theologies also shaped how European church leaders, theologians, and missionaries adopted an uncritical perception of the superiority of their own Eurocentric Christian theological ruminations and looked down on the cultures and religions of peoples beyond Europe as different, strange, and inferior to Christianity. In this regard, one is reminded of the late Edward Said's (1935–2003) devastating critique of how the "West"—that is, Europe—perceives Asia in terms of the "Orient" or the "East," encompassing the "Near East," "Middle East," and "Far East." Many church leaders, missionaries, theologians, and scholars of religion in Europe and North America continue to use these terms uncritically today to apply to different parts of Asia that are measured notionally "eastwards" from Europe as the center of civilization and knowledge, with the "Near East" of Asia being nearest to Europe and the "Far East" region of Asia being the furthest from Europe.

Implicit in this grid is Europe being perceived as the center of the world and the source of systematic, objective, critical, and rational knowledge; humane ideals; and superior insights. By contrast, the world beyond Europe was labeled as the "other" and filled with everything that is unsystematic, uncritical, subjective, strange and mysterious, uncivilized, backward, alien, devious, despotic, and ultimately undeveloped and inferior to European culture, religion, and way of life (see Said 1978, 42, 300–301). As Said explained, "Orientalism was ultimately a political vision of reality whose structure promoted the difference between the familiar (Europe, the West, 'us') and the strange (the Orient, the East, 'them')" (43). He reminded us that the production of knowledge is inextricably linked to power and domination, such that the ability to know and to represent arises from the ability to possess and control (see 86). He further pointed out that "Orientals were rarely seen or looked at; they were seen through, analyzed not as citizens, or even people, but as problems to be solved or confined or—as the colonial powers openly coveted their territory—taken over" (207).

While Said's acerbic diatribe was directed at European Orientalism toward Islam, Muslim-Christian relations, and how Europeans perceived the sociocultural, religious, and political realities of the Muslim world across Asia, his writings on Orientalism and postcolonialism have shaped much of the postcolonial critique of how European scholars study religion, culture, politics, and society beyond Europe and North America generally and in Asia in particular. More importantly, Said's insights highlight the insidious and uncritical colonial attitudes of European and North American theologians toward the varieties of theologizing that emerge from the majority world. For the longest time, theologians in North America and Europe have largely been insulated from the challenges posed by postcolonial ideas and insights. These theologians often uncritically assumed that their theologizing was universal and normative. They ignored issues of dominance arising from unequal power dynamics afforded by European imperialism and colonialism that not only produced, reproduced, and inscribed power but also deployed and controlled the articulation of as well as the beneficiaries of theological knowledge and insights.

Specifically, postcolonial insights and ideas challenge the structures and systems of unified meaning and knowledge, as well as deconstruct the so-called universal binaries or "us-versus-them" dualities—for example, West/East, primitive/civilized, sacred/secular, religious/civil, faith/heresy, universal/particular, cultured/barbarism, and so on—that many theologians in Europe and North America have taken for granted in their theologizing in favor of the myriad complex, multifaceted, and intersectional ways in which contemporary sociocultural and religious worlds are constructed amid much diversity and plurality. Postcolonial thinkers often point out the need to pay attention to whose voices are included and whose voices are excluded, as well as the impact of European colonial conquest and empire building on the unequal power dynamics in the articulation of knowledge and understanding.

Applying these broad postcolonial ideas to the task of theologizing, one should not be surprised at how European and North American theologians often uncritically ignore the impact of European colonial conquests and empire building in shaping the theological foundations of everything from missiology to liturgy, Christology to ecclesiology, and ethics to soteriology. They have often assumed the white male gaze and voice to be normative, not asking whose voices are being included and whose are being excluded. Ideas such as intersectionality in the task of theologizing are still novel, as are the challenges of majority and minority power dynamics within the complexities of multifaceted diversity and pluralism.

In response, Asian postcolonial theologians advocate for a postcolonial approach to doing theology in Asia that seeks to contest the legacy of European colonialism and imperialism across Asia, as well as deconstruct the uncritical acceptance of the normative superiority of European approaches and methods of doing theology. They stress the necessity of moving beyond these tainted approaches and the dominance of European methods in favor of modes of theologizing that take their cues from and respond to the realities and lived experiences of Asians on their own terms (Sugirtharajah 2006; Amaladoss 2014; Kwan 2014). Hence postcolonial theological ruminations take seriously the fact that the Asian peoples, with their rich diversity and various cultural and religious traditions as well as daily socioeconomic challenges, are not objects of theologizing by outsiders but rather subjects of theologizing with their own historical frames of reference, life experiences, and sociocultural contexts. Here we see how historical time periods in Europe with meaningful significance for European modes of theologizing (e.g., late antiquity, Middle Ages,

Renaissance, and Enlightenment) hold no meaningful significance at all for the contemporary lived experiences of Asian Christians (e.g., the Dalit Christians in India, Iban Catholics in Borneo, or East Timorese Catholics). Instead, as subjects of theologizing, we have to pay attention to how their lives, challenges, dreams, and hopes are being shaped by colonial history and legacy, caste, sociopolitical and economic systems, and majority-minority dynamics that we explored earlier in chapter 1.

I contend that as a new way of doing theology in the Asian milieu, the FABC's theological approach is inherently postcolonial, using Asian resources to transcend Eurocentric modes, responding to the specific concerns and needs of Asians that arise out of the concrete specificity of diverse Asian life experiences, and engaging with the sociocultural, religious, and political-economic realities of Asia, a continent that, in the words of the final statement of the first FABC Plenary Assembly, is facing a "swift and far-reaching transformation, a continent undergoing modernization and profound social change, along with secularization and the breakup of traditional societies" (FABC I, 4, in Rosales and Arévalo 1992, 13). This also means that in response to a continent that is changing rapidly, a postcolonial approach to doing Asian theology has to be dynamic and relational, perceiving sociocultural, religious, political, and economic realities across Asia not as closed and static realities but as constantly in a state of flux as a result of ongoing forces such as globalization and migration.

More significantly, the FABC's postcolonial theological approach explicitly rejects a mode of "doing theology in Asia" in favor of "doing Asian theology." In other words, the FABC's methodology takes the rich diversity and complexity of the lived experiences of the Asian peoples themselves as starting points for theologizing in Asia instead of conforming to an idealized, normative, or overarching and ahistorical framework that is built on abstract, philosophical, or intellectual ideas such as the European theological concepts of eternal law (*lex aeterna*) or natural law (*lex naturalis*); abstract metaphysical principles pertaining to God, revelation, and the Christian gospel; or even conciliar, papal, or doctrinal pronouncements. In contrast to the traditional discursive orientation of European scholastic theological methodologies that are invariably metaphysical in orientation, have traditionally focused on wisdom (*sapientia*) or rational knowledge (*scientia*), and are often detached from daily lived experiences, the FABC's postcolonial theologizing is people-centric in orientation, seeking to be shaped by as well as shaping the *lo cotidiano* of Asians in disparate sociocultural, economic, and religious milieus. Clearly, the FABC realizes that its theological responses cannot be presented as otherworldly, ignoring the suffering, pain, and injustices that Asians continue to experience as the ugly legacies of colonialism and imperialism.

An Intersectional Theology

The FABC has consistently noted that the Asian milieu is very different from Europe and the Americas, with their majority Christian presence and influence over society and culture, at least nominally. The Asian Catholic bishops know that they cannot presume a normative Eurocentric Christian framework for theologizing in the manner as may be carried out in Europe and the Americas, where a majority Christian environment for theologizing is often taken for granted. Instead, the FABC takes seriously how Asians generally and Asian Christians in particular are immersed within a threefold postcolonial Asian reality that is shaped by the *intersections* of the cultures and religions of Asia as well as the subaltern experiences of massive poverty and marginalization that define the socioeconomic realities of much of Asia.

The postcolonial paradigm of "intersectionality" that Kimberlé Crenshaw (1989) has articulated within the context of Black feminism is useful to explain the FABC's deliberate choice to pay attention to the *intersecting* impacts and implications of cultures, religions, and socioeconomic marginalization in its theological reflections. Specifically, Crenshaw argues that a Black woman's identity cannot be separated into distinct and independent identities of being Black and being a woman. Rather, her identity lies at the *intersection* of her two identities of being Black and being a woman, with both identities interacting on and reinforcing each other.

Applying Crenshaw's insights on intersectionality to the FABC's postcolonial theological approach, we see clearly how the FABC insists that the lived realities of Asians across postcolonial Asia cannot be compartmentalized into separate and distinct realities of culture, religion, and poverty. Instead, Asians generally and Asian Christians in particular live at the threefold intersections of culture, religion, and subaltern experiences of poverty and marginalization. As far as the FABC is concerned, one cannot separate the postcolonial Asian Christian experiences with Asian cultures, religions, and poverty into distinct and separate theological categories of inculturation, interreligious dialogue, or liberation theology.

It is clear that for the FABC, the intersectional experiences of Asian Christians as minority communities across postcolonial Asia call for theological responses that are shaped by the interplay and interactions between a trifecta of cultural, religious, and subaltern economic realities. This has led the FABC to develop its signature theological approach of threefold dialogue with the cultures, religions, and economic marginalization that Asian Christians experience as minority communities throughout postcolonial Asia. In other words, the FABC is unequivocal on the need to transcend an uncritical Christian exceptionalism and triumphalism to embrace intersectionality in its postcolonial theologizing that engages with the Asian peoples and their firsthand experiences of cultural diversity and religious pluralism, as well as challenging subaltern economic realities that include the endemic persistence of mass poverty, exploitative socioeconomic structures, and oppressive political systems that often deny basic human and democratic rights to the subaltern masses across postcolonial Asia.

Building on our discussion in this chapter, let me propose the following definition of the FABC's theological approach that I will use to anchor our exploration and critical evaluation of the FABC's theological responses to a variety of issues and challenges in the rest of this book:

> The FABC's theological approach is a postcolonial and intersectional theological approach that is rooted in and seeks to respond to the contemporary existential realities of Asian Christians as vibrant minority communities of faith amid their fellow neighbors who belong to the great religions of Asia, whose lives are shaped and impacted by the intersecting forces of cultures, religions, and subaltern socioeconomic realities. Hence the FABC's theologies may be defined as critical and pragmatic theologizing that embraces the diversity and pluralism of postcolonial Asia, as well as seeks to serve life in pluralistic Asia, promoting harmony among Asians across religious, ethnic-cultural, and socioeconomic classes in response to the hatred and violence that is destroying the social, cultural, and religious fabric of many parts of postcolonial Asia, as well as integrating the intersecting facets of intercultural, interreligious, and liberationist dimensions in its theological reflections.

I will unpack and explore the implications of this definition in the rest of the book as follows. Chapter 3 will explore how the FABC seeks to address the challenges of religious pluralism and diversity by rethinking the relationship between Christianity and the great religious traditions of Asia and critically considering their implications for doing theology in Asia. The Asian Catholic bishops realize that they cannot escape the reality that they are being challenged to reformulate their understanding of the relationship between Christianity and the resurgent growth of the great religions of Asia, recognizing the fact that religious pluralism is here to stay in postcolonial Asia, with Asian Christians remaining as minority communities of "little flocks" among the majority communities for the foreseeable future. In chapter 4, I will build on the insights of chapter 3 to discuss the FABC's new way of being church and doing Christian mission in postcolonial Asia, as well as the relationship between the church and the Reign of God, critically evaluating the FABC's innovative understanding of mission in postcolonial Asia as a threefold dialogue with the intersecting realities of Asian cultures, religions, and experiences of poverty and marginalization.

3

A "Little Flock" in Plurireligious Asia

When the Asian Catholic bishops take a critical look at the social-cultural, economic, political, and religious contexts of the daily life experiences of Asian Christians, they see that, with the exception of the Philippines or Timor-Leste, Asian Christians are not living in a world where Christianity is the dominant force that influences and shapes culture, ethics, politics, and society. As we have seen in the first chapter of this book, they cannot escape the reality that they are being challenged to reformulate their understanding of the relationship between Christianity and the resurgent Asian religions amid the *fact* and *reality* that religious pluralism is here to stay in postcolonial Asia. As Peter C. Phan puts it bluntly, they have to "take their Asianness seriously as the context of their being Christian" (2000, 218) because "it is in Asia that the question of religious pluralism is literally a matter of life and death," and more importantly, "the future of Asian Christianity hangs in balance depending on how religious pluralism is understood and lived out" (2003b, 117). While Phan acknowledges that they "must of course proclaim and live the Christian faith, the same faith handed down the ages," they nonetheless "should do so in the modalities conceived and born from within the Asian context," thereby enabling "the Churches *in* Asia [to] become truly *of* Asia" (2000, 219).

Moreover, in view of the reality, Phan further points out that "the report of the demise of Asian religions was premature and vastly exaggerated" and that many parts of Asia have witnessed a vigorous revival of Asian religions; therefore, Asian Christians "must come to terms with the fact that they are destined to remain for the foreseeable future a 'small remnant' who must journey with adherents of other religions toward the eschatological kingdom of God" (2000, 224).

Hence for the Asian Catholic bishops to "take their Asianness seriously as the context of their being Christian," as Peter C. Phan suggests, they would need to acknowledge that religious pluralism in postcolonial Asia is not a dilemma to be eradicated but a distinctive characteristic of being Asian and Christian. The Asian Catholic bishops know very well that unless they defend religious diversity and pluralism against exclusivist religious chauvinism, there will be no room at all for Christianity in a continent dominated by the great religions of Asia. Not surprisingly, the Federation of Asian Bishops' Conferences (FABC) accepts the reality that other religions define and dominate the social landscape in their homelands, with Asian Christians being the *pusillus grex*, or "little flock," in a sea of immense Asian religious diversity and plurality. As the FABC Office of Theological Concerns acknowledges, "The Christian communities in this part of the world, taken together, do not make up more than 2% of the entire population of Asia. Except for the Philippines, of whose 60 million population 83% are Catholic and 89% Christian, Christians are minorities in every Asian nation. The Church in Asia is truly a little flock, pusillus grex, an infinitesimal minority in an ocean of people who profess other religious faiths or belong to other religious traditions" (*Theses on the Local Church*, 8, in FABC Office of Theological Concerns 1991, 4).

In other words, because Asian Christianity will never dominate postcolonial Asia to the exclusion and extinction of other religions in the manner of medieval Christendom in Europe, it has to become truly immersed and rooted in the postcolonial Asian milieu for its survival and growth, as Peter C. Phan rightly notes. As religious minorities, Asian Christians have the daily experiences of being deeply immersed in the pluralistic religious Asian milieu, having been born into and living amid this religious diversity and pluralism. Moreover, many of them come from a "mixed" religious background, with extended family members following a variety of religious traditions. They live and interact daily with their family members, relatives, friends, and neighbors from other religious traditions, sharing with them the joys and sufferings as well as blessings and misfortunes of daily living. While many European and North American theologians and church leaders wax lyrical about the practice and achievements of interfaith dialogue in Europe and North America, where the great religions of the world are often viewed through an Orientalist lens as the minority and the exotic "other" vis-à-vis the dominant position of Christianity, Asian Christians live permanently amid the practitioners of these religions. And while theologians and church leaders in Europe and North America may invite representatives of these other religions to meet occasionally for dialogue and conversation, Asian Christians engage in a daily dialogue of life witness with these fellow Asian neighbors who are followers of the great religious traditions of Asia.

At the same time, the Asian Catholic bishops acknowledge the reality that Asian Christians' interactions with their fellow Asians who are adherents of other religious traditions are not always harmonious and peaceful. While Asia is often spoken of as the birthplace of the great religions of the world, including Christianity, many of these world religions are experiencing a resurgence of pride and exclusivist chauvinism in many parts of postcolonial

Asia, as we saw in the first chapter of this book. Thus Asian Christians also have firsthand experiences of fanatics and fundamentalists who reject the long history of religious diversity and pluralism in postcolonial Asia, seeking to impose their vision as normative through coercion, violence, or burdensome legislation—for example, the unwarranted pressure on Indian Christians to renounce Christianity, the simmering Muslim-Christian conflicts in Pakistan and elsewhere, Hindu violence against Christians in India, and the onerous restrictions in Malaysia on religious conversions or use of the term *Allah* for God.

Religious Pluralism from Vatican II to the FABC

To recapitulate from chapter 1, we saw how Vatican II, which was dominated by prelates from Europe and North America, glossed over, among many things, the challenges of diversity and pluralism in Asia at the council. In retrospect, it is clear that Vatican II adopted a very cautious and wary approach to the issue of religious diversity and pluralism in *Lumen gentium* (LG), as can be seen in its opening statement, which emphasizes the christocentric dimensions of salvation and the necessity of the proclamation of the gospel: "Christ is the light of all nations. Hence, this most sacred Synod, which has been gathered in the Holy Spirit, eagerly desires to shed on all men that radiance of His which brightens the countenance of the Church. This it will do by proclaiming the gospel to every creature" (LG 1, in Abbott 1966, 14–15). LG also insists on an ecclesiocentric grounding of *missio ad gentes*—that is, the church is necessary for salvation (Ecclesiam necessariam esse ad salutem, LG 14)—explaining that the church is "the universal sacrament of salvation" (universale salutis sacramentum) because the risen Christ is leading all peoples to the church (ut homines ad Ecclesiam perducat) and "through her joining them more closely to Himself" (LG 48, in Abbott 1966, 79).

LG's emphasis on the necessity of the church and the proclamation of the gospel for salvation is echoed in Vatican II's missionary decree, *Ad gentes* (AG), which reiterates the necessity of preaching the gospel, notwithstanding the possibility that salvation may be available by other channels: "Therefore, though God in ways known to Himself can lead those inculpably ignorant of the gospel to that faith without which it is impossible to please Him (Heb. 11:6), yet a necessity lies upon the Church (cf. 1 Cor. 9:16), and at the same time a sacred duty, to preach the gospel. Hence missionary activity today as always retains its power and necessity" (AG 7, in Abbott 1966, 593).

A breakthrough on the question of acknowledging the reality of religious diversity and pluralism came in Vatican II's *Declaration on the Relation of the Church to Non-Christian Religions*, *Nostra aetate* (NA), marking a paradigm shift in the church's understanding of other religions. In the two thousand–year history of the Catholic Church, NA is the first official church statement to recognize and accept other religions as entities that the church should respect and enter into dialogue with rather than suppressing them as evil and false. Eschewing the traditional terminology such as "pagan" (*paganus*), "idolatry" (*idolatria*), and "false religion" (*religio falsa*), the council fathers introduced a new atmosphere of respect and dialogue, recognizing the plurality and diversity of religions for the first time. On the one hand, NA unequivocally accepts that the manner of life and conduct, and precepts and doctrines, in other religions often contain gems of truth. On the other hand, NA also insists that the "fullness of religious life" (plenitudinem vitae religiosae) is to be found solely in Christ, and hence the church "proclaims and must ever proclaim Christ, 'the way, the truth, and the life' (John 1:6), in whom men find the fullness of religious life, and in whom God has reconciled all things to Himself"

(NA 2, in Abbott 1966, 662). NA proceeds to lay the foundations for dialogue as follows: "The Church therefore has this exhortation for her sons: prudently and lovingly, through dialogue and collaboration with the followers of other religions, and in witness of Christian faith and life, acknowledge, preserve, and promote the spiritual and moral goods found among these men, as well as the values in their society and culture" (NA 2, in Abbott 1966, 662–63).

In the ensuing decades after Vatican II, the Asian Catholic bishops of the FABC have gone beyond what their counterparts in Europe and North America have done, receiving and interpreting the documents of Vatican II in innovative ways in order to respond to the challenges of diversity and pluralism in postcolonial Asia, with its myriad cultures, religions, and peoples. In doing so, these Asian Catholic bishops have chosen to embrace the immense diversity and pluralism of postcolonial Asia, recognizing that such diversity and pluralism lie at the heart of what it means to be Asian. We also saw in the first chapter how many parts of contemporary postcolonial Asia are being torn apart by hatred and violence that are instigated by nationalist and religious extremism; the Asian Catholic Church is called to seek to heal the many political and religious conflicts that plague communities, societies, and cultures across Asia. In the next chapter of this book, we will examine how the FABC interprets and fleshes out NA's tentative call to dialogue more fully in its intersectional theology of threefold dialogue with cultures, religions, and the poor.

In contrast to the council fathers' hesitant response to religious diversity and pluralism at Vatican II, in its official statements and documents, the FABC has proceeded on the basis that the postcolonial Asian milieu—with its teeming masses and their rich diversity and pluralism of cultures, religions, and philosophical worldviews—requires a distinctively Asian approach that is sensitive to and responds to such diversity and pluralism beyond what the council fathers originally envisaged at Vatican II. According to the FABC, this distinctive Asian approach is needed in order to counteract the prejudicial stereotype, however unfair, that Christianity and the church are colonial relics and therefore alien to the Asian religious landscape. The FABC Theological Consultation of 1991 explains the dilemma facing the Asian Catholic bishops in the postcolonial Asian milieu as follows: "As a social institution the Church is perceived as a foreign body in its colonial origins while other world religions are not. The lingering colonial image survives in its traditional ecclesiastical structures and economic dependence on the west. . . . The Church is even sometimes seen as an obstacle or threat to national integration and to religious and cultural identity" (Theological Consultation, 13, in Rosales and Arévalo 1992, 337).

The Challenges of Pluralism in the Asian Milieu

The FABC has sought to articulate an intersectional approach for theologizing that seeks to respond to the challenges of diversity and pluralism in Asia—with its myriad cultures, religions, and peoples—with a distinctively Asian approach to doing theology that is sensitive to such diversity and pluralism. Thus at the Asian Bishops' Meeting (ABM) with Pope Paul VI in Manila (1970), the Asian Catholic bishops acknowledged that Asia is "a continent of ancient and diverse cultures, religions, histories and traditions, a region like Joseph's coat of many colors" (ABM 7, in Rosales and Arévalo 1992, 4; see FABC II, 7, in Rosales and Arévalo 1992, 30). Four years later, the first FABC Plenary Assembly, which gathered in Taipei, Taiwan, in 1974, recognized that the great religious traditions of Asia are "significant and positive elements in the economy of God's design and salvation. In them we recognize and respect profound spiritual and ethical meanings and values. Over many centuries, they have been the treasury of the religious experience of our ancestors, from which our contemporaries do not cease to draw light and strength. They have been (and continue to be) the authentic expression of the noblest longings of their hearts, and the home of their contemplation and prayer. They have helped to give shape to the histories and cultures of our nations" (FABC I, 14, in Rosales and Arévalo 1992, 14).

As a follow-up to FABC I, the second FABC Bishops' Institute for Social Action (BISA II) put forward the following statement on pluralism that would undergird subsequent discussions on it in the various FABC plenary assemblies and FABC bishops' institutes: "Pluralism is a necessity once we work through the mediation of secular analysis and worldviews. This pluralism should not be a threat to our Christian unity, but on the contrary, a positive and creative sign that our unity is deeper than whatever the concrete technical analysis or viewpoints might show: a genuine value that emphasizes unity in diversity" (BISA II, 10, in Rosales and Arévalo 1992, 204). Without a doubt, the FABC perceives diversity and pluralism in positive terms: "Peace and harmony in Asian societies, composed as they are of many cultural, ethnic and linguistic groups, would require recognition of legitimate pluralism and respect for all the groups. Unity, peace and harmony are to be realized in diversity" (Bishops' Institute for Interreligious Affairs [BIRA] IV/11, 15, in Rosales and Arévalo 1992, 321).

For the FABC, diversity and plurality are to be not gotten rid of but "rejoiced over and promoted" (BIRA IV/11, 15, in Rosales and Arévalo 1992, 321). In this regard, the FABC's Office of Theological Concerns explains the relationship between pluralism and dialogue in its landmark 1987 document *Theses on Interreligious Dialogue* as follows: "In the course of the last two thousand years the Church has encountered and dialogued with various peoples, cultures and religions, with varying levels of success. Today, however, especially in Asia, in the context of the Great Religions, which are in a process of revival and renewal, the Church is aware of a markedly different situation. We do not ask any longer about the relationship of the Church to other cultures and religions. We are rather searching for the place and role of the Church in a religiously and culturally pluralistic world" (0.8, in FABC Office of Theological Concerns 1987, 3). On this basis, the Indian theologian Lorenzo Fernando observes that from its inception, the FABC has eschewed all forms of religious exclusivism, perceiving religious pluralism as an innate and unique aspect of the Asian socioreligious landscape (2000, 864–69).

In its articulation of an Asian theology of religious pluralism, the FABC is careful to take as its foundation two key insights on the Holy Spirit from the documents of Vatican II. In AG, the council fathers noted, "Doubtless, the Holy Spirit was already at work in the world before Christ was glorified" (AG 4, in Abbott 1966, 587). This idea was subsequently developed in the *Pastoral Constitution on the Church in the Modern World, Gaudium et spes* (GS), to encompass the Holy Spirit offering the possibility of salvation for all of humanity: "For since Christ died for all men, and since the ultimate vocation of man is in fact one, and divine, we ought to believe that the Holy Spirit in a manner known only to God offers to every man the possibility of being associated with this paschal mystery" (GS 22, in Abbott 1966, 221–22). Building on these two important theological insights, the FABC stresses that the religious traditions of Asia are "expressions of the presence of God's Word and of the universal action of his Spirit in them" (Theological Consultation, 43, in Rosales and Arévalo 1992, 344), revealing the "inescapable truth that God's Spirit is at work in all religious traditions" (BIRA IV/12, 7, in Rosales and Arévalo 1992, 326). On this point, the FABC makes the following groundbreaking observation: "It has been recognized since the time of the apostolic Church, and stated clearly again by the Second Vatican Council, that the Spirit of Christ is active outside the bounds of the visible Church. God's saving grace is not limited to members of the Church, but is offered to every person. His grace may lead some to accept baptism and enter the Church, but it cannot be presumed that this must always be the case. His ways are mysterious and unfathomable, and no one can dictate the direction of His grace" (BIRA II, 12, in Rosales and Arévalo 1992, 115; see BIRA IV/1, 10, in Rosales and Arévalo 1992, 249). The third FABC Plenary Assembly urges Asian Christians to "listen to the Spirit at work in the many communities of believers who live and experience their own faith, who share and celebrate it in their own social, cultural and religious history," accompanying them "in a common pilgrimage toward the ultimate goal, in relentless quest for the Absolute," and becoming "sensitively attuned to the work of the Spirit in the resounding symphony of Asian communion" (FABC III, 8.2, in Rosales and Arévalo 1992, 57).

The FABC recognizes that the "great religions of Asia with their respective creeds, cults and codes reveal to us diverse ways of responding to God whose Spirit is active in all peoples and cultures" (BIRA IV/7, 12, in Rosales and Arévalo 1992, 310). It is "the same spirit, who has been active in the incarnation, life, death and resurrection of Jesus and in the Church, who was active among all peoples before the Incarnation and is active among the nations, religions and peoples of Asia today" (BIRA IV/3, 6, in Rosales and Arévalo 1992, 259). On this basis, the FABC speaks of tapping into the movement across Asia "among peoples of various faiths to break down traditional barriers of division and hostility, and their initiative to reach out to neighbors of other faiths in a spirit of love, friendship, harmony and collaboration," and "discerning the hand of God" in "all these aspirations, movements and initiatives" (BIRA IV/11, 5, in Rosales and Arévalo 1992, 318–19). Commenting on this, Felix Wilfred writes, "Any work of mission which does not recognize what God has been doing with a people, with a country and continent and with their history, is simply and purely arrogance vis-à-vis God's own bounteous gifts. . . . Triumphalism and exclusivism of any kind are diametrically opposed to spirituality.

They fail to recognize and appreciate the thousand flowers God has let grow, flourish and blossom in the garden of the world; they fail to acknowledge in practice the presence and working of the Spirit in the life and history of peoples" (1990, 590).

The radical nature of the FABC's understanding of religious pluralism can be seen in the final statement of the 1995 FABC Hindu-Christian Dialogue, which makes the following unequivocal point on religious pluralism as constitutive of the postcolonial Asian reality:

> Beyond the extremes of inclusivism and exclusivism, pluralism is accepted in resonance with the constitutive plurality of reality. Religions, as they are manifested in history, are complementary perceptions of the ineffable divine mystery, the God-beyond-God. All religions are visions of the divine mystery. No particular religion can raise the claim of being the norm for all others. We religious believers are co-pilgrims, who share intimate spiritual experiences and reflections with one another with concern and compassion, with genuine openness to truth and the freedom of spiritual seekers (*sadhakas*). In this process we become increasingly sensitive to human suffering and collaborate in promoting justice, peace and ecological wholeness. (BIRA V/3, 6, in Eilers 1997, 157–58)

This rejection of all forms of religious exclusivism echoes an earlier statement by BIRA IV: "When various religious groups lay absolute claim to truth, aggressive militancy and divisive proselytism follow and, in their wake, bitter religious divisions" (BIRA IV/4, 4, in Rosales and Arévalo 1992, 300).

In response to critics of religious pluralism who raise the specter of unbridled theological relativism or subjectivism, the FABC Office of Theological Concerns explains that recognition of religious pluralism does not necessarily lead to an acceptance of subjectivism or relativism:

> Pluralism need not always entail a radical subjectivism or relativism, in the sense of claiming that all points of view are equally valid. However, it is also true that the dawn of pluralistic, democratic, modern societies has paved the way to excessive individualism and subjectivism, and a consequent relativizing of all reality. Thus, today there are persons and groups who hold all reality to be relative. For such persons or groups, pluralism means relativism, in the sense that they claim all points of view are equally valid. *Such philosophical or theological positions are to be rejected; and, in fact, all the major Asian religions condemn such relativizing of reality, especially the relativizing of basic human values.* However, just because certain persons and groups are misled in their search for truth, and just because they tend to perceive pluralism as relativism, or just because they tend to relativize all reality, we cannot conclude that all pluralism leads to relativism. (*Methodology: Asian Christian Theology,* 1.1, in Eilers 2002, 334; emphasis added)

A Commitment and Service to Life in Pluralistic Asia

From the foregoing discussion, it is clear to us that the Asian Catholic bishops are very much at home with the diversity and pluralism of postcolonial Asia, steering away from all forms of religious exclusivism in favor of working within the pluralism of the Asian milieu, with its diverse cultures and religions. Not surprisingly, while others may consider the diversity and pluralism of postmodern Europe and North America as challenges that Christianity has to confront and overcome, as far as the Asian Catholic bishops are concerned, the challenge is rather how Asian Christianity could be at home within these two things. Out of a holistic perspective of living in postcolonial Asia that perceives God's Spirit as actively engaging in the diverse and pluralistic Asian milieu, we see the FABC calling for a *commitment and service to life* in postcolonial Asia. Indeed, the final statement of the 1994 FABC International Theological Colloquium begins simply as follows: "Life. Vibrant life pulsating in the fecundity of Asia" (*Being Church in Asia*, 1, in Eilers 1997, 217).

The FABC elaborates on its call for a commitment and service to life in postcolonial Asia in the final statement of the sixth FABC Plenary Assembly, with its theme of "Christian Discipleship in Asia Today: Service to Life," as well as the first two sections of its final statement, entitled "25 Years of FABC Commitment to Life" and "A Vision of Life amid Asian Realities." FABC VI makes the following powerful statement about service life in Asia: "We Asians are searching not simply for the meaning of life but for life itself. We are striving and struggling for life because it is a task and a challenge. But life is a gift too, a mystery, because our efforts to achieve it are far too short of the ultimate value of life. We speak of life as a *becoming*—a growing into, a journeying to life and to the source of life" (FABC VI, 9, in Eilers 1997, 5). FABC VI unpacks this statement by highlighting "a vision of unity in diversity, a communion of life among diverse peoples" within this "vision of holistic life, life that is achieved and entrusted to every person and every community of persons, regardless of gender, creed or culture, class, or color" (FABC VI, 10, in Eilers 1997, 5). It also describes its approach and goals as follows:

> Our solidarity requires a resolve *to work with our*
> *Asian sisters and brothers in liberating our societies*
> *from whatever oppresses and degrades human life and*

creation, most especially from sin. . . . Serving life demands
communion with every woman and man seeking and
struggling for life in the way of Jesus' solidarity with
humanity. With our Asian sisters and brothers, we will
strive to foster communion among Asian peoples who
are threatened by glaring economic, social, and political
imbalances. With them we will explore ways of utilizing
the gifts of our diverse religions, cultures, and languages to
achieve a richer and deeper Asian unity. We build bridges
of solidarity and reconciliation with peoples of other faiths
and will join hands with everyone in Asia in forming a true
community of creation. (FABC VI, 14.2, in Eilers 1997, 8;
emphasis added)

Moreover, FABC VI also insists on the need to "pitch our tents in
the midst of all humanity" so as "to immerse ourselves in Asia's
cultures of poverty and deprivation, from whose depths the aspirations for love and life are most poignant and compelling," because
serving life "demands communion with every woman and man
seeking and struggling for life, in the way of Jesus' solidarity with
humanity" (FABC VI, 14.2, in Eilers 1997, 8). It also uses the powerful symbolism of Jesus's foot washing to underlie its call for
commitment and service to life: "We join Jesus in serving life by
washing the feet of our neighbors" (FABC VI, 14.3, in Eilers 1997, 9).
    The first FABC International Theological Colloquium articu-
lates the close connection between doing theology and serving
life in postcolonial Asia in its final statement, *Being Church in
Asia*, as follows:

We see the work of theology in Asia as a *service to life.* It
has *to reflect systematically on themes that are important
to the common journey of life with other peoples in Asia*, to
the life of Christians and their churches in Asia, and to the

work of the Asian episcopal conferences. To do this service in a way that is pastorally relevant and fruitful to the life, spirituality and mission of the disciple-community, *theology has to start from below,* from the underside of history, from the perspective of those who struggle for life, love, justice and freedom. The life-long experiences of living the Christian faith by the various churches in their Asian context are the starting points. *Theologizing thus becomes more than faith seeking understanding, but faith fostering life and love, justice and freedom.* It is in this way that theology becomes a dynamic process giving meaning to and facilitating the Asian journey to life. It becomes part of the process of becoming and being Church in Asia. (48–50, in Eilers 1997, 226; emphasis added)

We see from this statement in *Being Church in Asia* that the FABC is insistent that the task of theologizing in postcolonial Asia should be carried out *together with* the Asian peoples and in solidarity and empathy with their daily life experiences rather than merely *about* the Asian peoples or *for* their benefit. As Felix Wilfred reminds us, "What we are with the people is more important than what we do for them" (1998, 132). Moreover, the statement's call to make a personal commitment to the Asian peoples and their life experiences entails more than mere sympathy or occasional encounters with their daily lives. Rather, it calls for a deep immersion and experiential participation in their lives, not as outsiders who drop by sporadically to visit and then leave, but as insiders who remain bound in solidarity and empathy with them. Such a commitment and service to life may be understood from a twofold perspective—an explicit *epistemological* perspective that enables one to understand better the Asian peoples and their life experiences and, more importantly, an underlying *theological* perspective that recognizes the divine presence and workings in the daily lives of the Asian peoples. This underlying theological perspective is deeply rooted in the incarnation, earthly ministry, death, and resurrection of Jesus, revealing the divine solidarity and empathy with humanity, especially the poor and marginalized, as well as the divine participation in the experiences of pain and suffering in their daily lives. Hence one could say that the experiences of daily living (*lo cotidiano*) are the privileged loci where God is to be found and encountered because God has made a deliberate choice to be identified with humanity, especially the poor and marginalized.

On this basis, the FABC is of the view that Jesus Christ is to be encountered in postcolonial Asia within the specificity of the Asian people's subaltern lived realities and especially in the midst of the poor and marginalized. As the fifth Plenary Assembly of the FABC explains, the Christian community "must live in *companionship*, as true *partners* with all Asians as they pray, work, struggle and suffer for a better human life, and as they search for the meaning of human life and progress" because "the human person created in Christ, redeemed by Christ and united by Christ to himself is the way for the Church, the Church must walk along with him/her in human solidarity" (FABC V, 6.2, in Rosales and Arévalo 1992, 283). BISA VII elaborates on this point in the following manner: "The Lord of History is at work in that world of poverty. Seeing the Lord in the poor, making sense out of his action among them, discerning the direction of his action among them—this we felt deeply within us was the more specific challenge we have to face" (BISA VII, 20, in Rosales and Arévalo 1992, 233).

The Quest for Harmony in the Pluralistic Asian Milieu

The FABC's quest for harmony in the pluralistic Asian milieu is rooted in its belief that "there is an Asian approach to reality, a world-view, wherein the whole is the sum-total of the web of relationships and interaction of the various parts with each other, in a word, *harmony*, a word which resonates with all Asian cultures" (*Asian Christian Perspectives on Harmony*, 6, in Eilers 1997, 298). BIRA IV/11 unpacks this using the traditional Asian vision of a cosmic harmony binding humanity, nature, and the universe: "When we look into our traditional cultures and heritages, we note that they are inspired by a vision of unity. The universe is perceived as an organic whole with the web of relations knitting together each and every part of it. The nature and the human are not viewed as antagonistic to each other, but as chords in a universal symphony" (BIRA IV/11, 6, in Rosales and Arévalo 1992, 319).

The FABC speaks of harmony as "the spiritual pursuit of the totality of reality in its infinite diversity and radical unity" that "evolves by respecting the otherness of the other and by acknowledging its significance in relation to the totality" because "the ultimate ground of being is unity-in-plurality, the divergent forms of reality are perceived in the convergent rhythm that harmonizes them" (BIRA V/4, 6, in Eilers 1997, 157). The FABC also explains that despite "religious, ethnic, linguistic and cultural diversity, one can perceive a unity of values and perceptions" that is epitomized in the spirit of harmony because "harmony, in the created universe, within the human family, and internalized in the individual person, has for centuries been an ideal to which peoples of the region have striven" (*Harmony among Believers of Living Faiths*, 5, in Eilers 1997, 174).

More significant is the FABC's powerful insistence that "the way of harmony does not unfold through aggressive indoctrination, which distorts reality" (BIRA V/3, 7, in Eilers 1997, 158). In the final statement of its sixth Plenary Assembly, the FABC speaks of the experience of harmony within an overarching and holistic vision of unity in the Asian milieu: "We envision a life *with integrity and dignity, a life of compassion* for the multitudes, especially for the poor and needy. It is a life of *solidarity* with every form of life and of *sensitive care* for the earth. . . . At the heart of our vision of life is the Asian *reverential sense of mystery and of the sacred*, a spirituality that regards life as sacred and discovers the Transcendent and its gifts even in mundane affairs, in tragedy or victory, in brokenness or wholeness" (FABC VI, 10, in Eilers 1997, 5; see also the FABC Office of Theological Concerns' statement *The Spirit at Work in Asia Today*, in Eilers 2002, 237–327). This builds on the earlier statement made by the fourth FABC Plenary Assembly: "Asian religious cultures see human beings, society and the whole universe as intimately related and interdependent. Fragmentation and division contradict this vision" (FABC IV, 3.1.10, in Rosales and Arévalo 1992, 181).

It is significant that the FABC undergirds its theology of harmony in a vision of cosmic harmony and unity that accepts the pluralism and diversity of the Asian religio-cultural traditions as positive and rich expressions of the mystery of the divine plan of creation:

When we look into our traditional cultures and heritages, we note that they are inspired by a vision of unity. The universe is perceived as an organic whole with the web of relations knitting together each and every part of it. The nature and the human are not viewed as antagonistic to each other, but as chords in a universal symphony. The whole reality is maintained in unity through a universal rhyme (*Rta; Tao*). This unity of reality is reflected in the human person in that his senses, consciousness and spirit are organically interlinked, one flowing into the other. When this unity and harmony are manifested in inter-human relationship of justice, order and righteousness, it is considered *dharmic (dharma, dhamma)*. (BIRA IV/11, 6, in Rosales and Arévalo 1992, 319)

As far as the FABC is concerned, the theological paradigm of harmony is well positioned to act as the common underlying foundation for communication amid much diversity and pluralism because it is authentically Christian yet quintessentially Asian. For the FABC, it appears "to constitute in a certain sense the intellectual and affective, religious and artistic, personal and societal soul of both persons and institutions in Asia" (BIRA IV/1, 13, in Rosales and Arévalo 1992, 249). BIRA V/2 puts forward the following inclusive vision of harmony: "Harmony can be perceived and realized at various levels: Harmony in oneself as personal integration of body and mind; harmony with the Cosmos, not only living in harmony with nature, but sharing nature's gift equitably to promote harmony among peoples; harmony with others, accepting, respecting and appreciating each one's cultural, ethnic and religious identity, building community in freedom and fellowship; harmony in our collaborations as a means of promoting harmony for all in the world; and finally harmony with God or the Absolute or whatever we perceive as the ultimate goal of life" (BIRA V/2, 3.2, in Eilers 1997, 151).

In response to critics who challenge the naivete of harmony, the FABC unequivocally rejects the simplistic understanding of it as the mere absence of strife: "Harmony is not simply the absence of strife, described as 'live and let live.' The test of true harmony lies in the acceptance of diversity as richness" (BIRA IV/11, 15, in Rosales and Arévalo 1992, 321). The FABC goes on to explain, "Harmony does not consist in leveling off differences in order to arrive at consensus at any cost. Avoiding controversies and bypassing disagreements do not pave the way to harmony. To say that all religions are the same is simplistic and does not promote honest dialogue, but to argue that religions do not meet at all would block any creative interaction" (BIRA V/3, 7, in Eilers 1997, 158).

The FABC further notes that "Christianity teaches a threefold harmony: harmony with God, among humans, and with the whole universe. Union with a personal God is viewed as the source of all genuine harmony" (BIRA V/4, 5, in Eilers 1997, 164). From the Christian perspective, it is also divinely inspired because "God is the source and summit of all harmony. He is the foundation and the fulfillment of it" (*Asian Christian Perspectives on Harmony*, 5.1.1.4, in Eilers 1997, 288). The FABC further grounds its theology of harmony in the harmonious unity of the Trinity: "The marvelous mystery of unity and communion of the Trinity is a model as well as a powerful challenge in our efforts to create harmony in all areas of life" (BIRA IV/11, 7, in Rosales and Arévalo 1992, 319). This is further elaborated by the FABC Office of Theological Concerns as follows: "The harmony of the universe finds its origin in the one Creator God, and human harmony should flow from the communion of Father and Son in the Spirit, and ought to be continually nourished by the 'circumincession' (*perichoresis*) in divine life" (*Asian Christian Perspectives on Harmony*, 4.11.3, in Eilers 1997, 285). These Trinitarian and cosmic perspectives express powerfully a divine vision of harmony that "acknowledges the sacredness of nature and invites us to live in harmony with nature and to foster its growth" (BIRA IV/12, 33, in Rosales and Arévalo 1992, 330) and is "geared ultimately to the well-being and peace of the universe and humankind" (BIRA IV/11, 21, in Rosales and Arévalo 1992, 322).

Harmony, Environment, and Ecology

An important development that emerges from the FABC's theology of harmony is how harmony undergirds the FABC's theological reflections on the care for the environment and ecology. Peter C. Phan points out that the FABC is "probably the first official church body to be deeply concerned about ecology" (2018, 295). He explains that the FABC is unique and original in rooting its theology of care for the environment in its vision of fourfold harmony "with God, with oneself, with others, and with nature" (296).

As early as 1986, when care for the environment and ecology had yet to emerge as an important theological question in Europe and the Americas, the fourth Plenary Assembly of the FABC posed this question for reflection and action: "Asian religious cultures see human beings, society and the whole universe as intimately related and interdependent. Fragmentation and division contradict this vision. In the light of the Gospel, how does the Christian base the struggle for peace, justice and wholeness in this holistic vision provided by the ancient religions of Asia?" (FABC IV, 3.1.10, in Rosales and Arévalo 1992, 181). What is noteworthy here is how the Asian Catholic bishops draw inspiration from Asian religious cultures to ask how this "holistic vision" can challenge Asian Christians to approach this issue in an Asian manner. FABC IV's challenge is subsequently taken up by two meetings of BIRA—BIRA IV/11 and BIRA IV/12.

Meeting in Sukabumi, Indonesia, in 1988, BIRA IV/11 explores the "ecological question" through the lens of "harmony and balance of the natural environment" in relation to human life, noting that "the destiny of humankind is inextricably bound up with the way they cultivate the earth and share its resources" and elaborating on this close interconnection between harmony, environment, and ecology as follows: "Harmony and peace call for respect for the earth. She is the mother of whose dust we are made and to whose womb we shall all return. The usurpation of the fruit of the earth by some and deprivation of others of the same results in the rupture of harmony among peoples" (BIRA IV/11, 13, in Rosales and Arévalo 1992, 320). In response to this issue, BIRA IV/11 makes the following pastoral recommendation:

> Respect for nature and compassion for all living things are ingrained in the Asian religions and cultural traditions. Today in Asia owing to many factors, the natural environment with which man should be in harmony is being wantonly destroyed through deforestation, industrial pollution, depositing of nuclear wastes, etc. Christian life and witness should manifest greater sensitivity to nature and to all sentiments. Hence we recommend that Christians join forces and cooperate with all movements of followers of other religions and secular groups engaged in maintaining balance and harmony in our ecosystem, and protecting nature and its riches from destruction. (BIRA IV/11, recommendation 2, in Rosales and Arévalo 1992, 323)

BIRA IV/12, which met in Hua Hin, Thailand, in 1991, takes up the gauntlet that was thrown down by BIRA IV/11. First, it highlights how Asian religious traditions acknowledge the sacredness of nature and invite Asians to live in harmony with nature and contrasts this with human greed, which leads to the misuse and plundering of nature, posing a serious threat to both humans and the world that they live in (BIRA IV/12, 33, in Rosales and Arévalo 1992, 330). BIRA IV/12 then makes the case that Asians of all faith persuasions have a duty to care for and protect the environment, grounding this within the framework of harmony: "Believers in any place are called to come together in silence and love before creation, to accept the God-given order and harmony of nature, to counteract the forces of exploitation and ruin. Harmony with nature brings harmony of hearts and harmony in human relationships" (BIRA IV/12, 34, in Rosales and Arévalo 1992, 331).

Commenting on the insights of BIRA IV/11 and BIRA IV/12, *Asian Christian Perspectives on Harmony* is able to draw attention to how disharmony negatively affects the environment and ecology, citing as examples the indiscriminate logging and deforestation, soil erosion, despoiling of watershed areas, pollution of wetlands and fishing zones caused by the use of coastal waters for waste dumping, ruin of farmland, rise in deaths as a result of harmful air pollution, and toxic poisoning of slum dwellers in Bhopal, India, and the fatal toxic spills in South Korea and Thailand (*Asian Christian Perspectives on Harmony*, 1.3, in Eilers 1997, 238). It further develops the insights of BIRA IV/11 and BIRA IV/12 as follows: "Harmony with nature requires humans to reject an anthropocentric view of the universe, and to respect all of creation as the *vestigia Dei*. This respect generates a harmony which reflects God's providential love for his creatures. Humanity is called to discover in the universe God's very presence (Ps. 104, 109), and to cocreate with him, making the earth more fruitful" (*Asian Christian Perspectives on Harmony*, 5.1.1.3, in Eilers 1997, 287).

The robust foundations that BIRA IV/11 and BIRA IV/12 provided paved the way for the sixth FABC Plenary Assembly, which met in Manila in 1995, to articulate an elaborate theology of care for the environment way before this issue would become mainstream in theological discussions in Europe and North America. After identifying and denouncing the "forces of death" across Asia (FABC VI, 7, in Eilers 1997, 3–4) and calling attention to "movements for the protection of the environment and ecosystem linked to justice" (FABC VI, 8, in Eilers 1997, 4), FABC VI proceeded to build its theology of the environment in a vision of a "holistic life" of "solidarity with every form of life and of sensitive care for the earth," uniting Asians among themselves and "with the whole of creation into one community of life." More importantly, it grounded its theological vision in "the Asian reverential sense of mystery and of the sacred" that draws everyone "to experience harmony and inner peace," which "infuses ethics into all of creation" (FABC VI, 10, in Eilers 1997, 5). FABC VI calls on all Asian Christians to confront and act against all forms of death-dealing realities, including "the destruction of eco-systems" and "the tampering with life," arguing, "As disciples we cannot serve both life and death! . . . We in Asia today must prophesy on behalf of the God of life. Refusal to prophesy and speak against the forces of death is to fail in serving life!" (FABC VI, 14.3, in Eilers 1997, 9). Finally, FABC VI urges everyone to seek life and collaborate against the destruction of the environment and ecology: "Ecology is once again brought to our pastoral attention. And urgently so, since we see in the countries of Asia the continuing and unabated destruction of our environment. . . . Life, especially in a third world setting, is sacrificed at the altar of short term economic gains. The Lord, the Giver of Life, calls our discipleship in Asia into a question on the time bomb issue of ecology. Choosing life requires our discipleship to discern and act with other faiths and groups against the forces of ecological destruction" (FABC VI, 15.4, in Eilers 1997, 11).

4

A New Way of Being Church in Asia

Looking at the resurgence of religious vitality in postcolonial Asia among the adherents of the great religious traditions of Asia, it is clear that religious pluralism poses a significant challenge to the twofold task of constructing an ecclesiology for the Asian context and doing Christian mission in Asia. First, how should the Federation of Asian Bishops' Conferences (FABC) respond to the resurgence and renewed vitality of other religious majorities in postcolonial Asia, as well as the challenges and opportunities of religious pluralism? Second, how should the FABC embark on the twofold task of constructing a distinctive Asian ecclesiology and doing Christian mission in Asia that would be sensitive to the rich diversity of cultures and plurality of religious traditions?

In this chapter, I propose that the FABC has proceeded on the basis that the postcolonial Asian continent requires a distinctively Asian ecclesiology, a "new way of being church" that can be summarized as follows: the postcolonial Asian church is called to be a "communion of communities" that is oriented toward the task of doing Christian mission as an intersectional threefold dialogue with Asian cultures (inculturation), religions (interreligious dialogue), and the subaltern realities of poverty, exploitation, and marginalization (liberation theology) with the principal goal of seeking to bring about the Reign of God in Asia. What is new, original, and innovative in the FABC's approach is how it is able to *integrate* the threefold *intersectional* dimensions of cultures, religions, and subaltern experiences of poverty and marginalization in an *interactive* and holistic manner. In this respect, Peter C. Phan observes, "It is true as well that liberation theology is the original contribution of the Latin American church (with an emphasis on liberation from economic poverty) and that inculturation has been a deep concern of African Christianity (with a stress on liberation from cultural and anthropological domination). Nevertheless, it is the Asian Catholic churches that have consistently, insistently, and officially adopted the three dialogues in all their reciprocal and intrinsic connections as the overall agenda for pastoral ministry, church life, and spirituality, so much so that 'dialogue' has become synonymous with the new-way-of-being-church in Asia" (2018, 16).

The Asian Church as a "Communion of Communities"

In the first decade of its existence, the FABC focused its attention on defining and exploring the implications of the "local church." This term was specifically defined by the first FABC Plenary Assembly as "the realization and enfleshment of the Body of Christ in a given people, a given place and time" (FABC I, 10, in Rosales and Arévalo 1992, 14) that is "incarnate in a people, a church indigenous and inculturated" (FABC I, 12, in Rosales and Arévalo 1992, 14).[1] Beginning in the 1980s, the FABC expanded its ecclesiology to encompass the church as communion: "The Church is at its deepest level a *communion* (*koinonia*) rooted in the life of the

Trinity, and thus in its essential reality a sacrament (*mysterium et sacramentum*) of the loving self-communication of God and the graced response of redeemed mankind in faith, hope and love" (FABC III, 7.1, in Rosales and Arévalo 1992, 56). This communion is expressed in a new understanding of the Asian church as "a communion of committed disciples—be they clergy or laity—working for the liberation of Asia" (FABC IV, 4.1.3, in Rosales and Arévalo 1992, 191). A major paradigm shift occurred at the fifth FABC Plenary Assembly in Bandung, Indonesia, which put forward a new theological paradigm of the postcolonial Asian church as a "communion of communities": "The Church in Asia will have to be a communion of communities, where laity, Religious and clergy recognize and accept each other as sisters and brothers. They are called together by the word of God which, regarded as a quasi-sacramental presence of the Risen Lord, leads them to form small Christian communities (e.g., neighborhood groups, Basic Ecclesial Communities and 'covenant' communities). There, they pray and share together the Gospel of Jesus, living it in their daily lives as they support one another and work together, united as they are 'in one mind and heart'" (FABC V, 8.1.1, in Rosales and Arévalo 1992, 287). This understanding was reinforced by the sixth FABC Plenary Assembly in Manila, which reiterated the need for the postcolonial Asian church to move toward "a new way of being Church, a Church that is committed to becoming 'a community of communities,' and a credible sign of liberation and salvation" (FABC VI, 3, in Eilers 1997, 3). The fifth Plenary Assembly in Bandung also explained that this new way of being Church as a "communion of communities" is marked by three characteristics: it is participatory, dialogical, and prophetic.

First, the postcolonial Asian church is called to be "a participatory Church where the gifts that the Holy Spirit gives to all the faithful—lay, Religious, and cleric alike—are recognized and activated, so that the Church may be built up and its mission realized"

(FABC V, 8.1.2, in Rosales and Arévalo 1992, 287). Second, it is summoned to be "a Church that faithfully and lovingly witnesses to the Risen Lord and reaches out to people of other faiths and persuasions in a dialogue of life toward the integral liberation of all" (FABC V, 8.1.3, in Rosales and Arévalo 1992, 287–88). This echoes the insight of the first FABC Plenary Assembly, which views the Asian "church in continuous, humble and loving dialogue with the living traditions, the cultures, the great religions—in brief, with all the life-realities of the people in whose midst it has sunk its roots deeply and whose history and life it gladly makes its own" (FABC I, 12, in Rosales and Arévalo 1992, 14). Third, it is challenged to be "a leaven of transformation in this world and serves as a prophetic sign daring to point beyond this world to the ineffable Kingdom that is yet fully to come" (FABC V, 8.1.4, in Rosales and Arévalo 1992, 288). Following the Bandung meeting, the FABC has gone a step further in implementing its vision of bringing about a "new way of being church" by developing what it calls an Asian Integral Pastoral Approach towards a New Way of Being Church in Asia (AsIPA; see Eilers 1997, 107–11, 137–39; and Eilers 2002, 107–12). For the FABC, AsIPA is "a participatory way of being Church" where the "whole community of the faithful are enabled to actively share in the integral, global vision and mission of Christ, in the multidimensional context of Asia" (Eilers 1997, 108).

An Asian Approach to Doing Christian Mission

From the very beginning, the FABC has consistently asserted that at the heart of the postcolonial Asian church's self-understanding is the Asian approach to doing Christian mission as a threefold dialogue with the cultures, religions, and poor of Asia with the goal of bringing about the Reign of God in Asia. This understanding of mission in postcolonial Asia as dialogue is rooted in the

FABC's incarnational ecclesiology, articulated at its inaugural Plenary Assembly, which met in Taipei, Taiwan, in 1974 on the theme "Evangelization in Modern Day Asia." FABC I speaks of the local church as "the realization and enfleshment of the Body of Christ in a given people, a given place and time" (FABC I, 10, in Rosales and Arévalo 1992, 14) that is "incarnate in a people, a church indigenous and inculturated" (FABC I, 12, in Rosales and Arévalo 1992, 14). In turn, this incarnational ecclesiology provides the foundation for an incarnational theology of Christian mission that embraces the immense diversity and pluralism of the postcolonial Asian milieu, recognizing that such diversity and pluralism lie at the heart of what it means to be Asian.

More specifically, the FABC perceives postcolonial Asia's cultural, religious, and socioeconomic realities as very much intertwined with each other, leading to the inescapable conclusion that the religiosity of the Asian peoples is not primarily individualistic in orientation; rather, it has significant social, public, and ecological consequences:

> Culture, religion and society are interdependent, interacting and mutually transforming. In our Asian continent, which is the cradle for all the great world religions, culture and religion are integrated. Religion is the dynamic element of culture. Together they form the religio-cultural system which interacts with the socio-economic-political system of society, permeating every sphere of human life. Asian poverty is not a purely economic concept, neither is its religiosity merely cultural. Poverty and religiosity are interwoven in the Asian ethos, in such a way that at a certain point they seem to coalesce in order to procreate the specific character of Asia. (Bishops' Institute for Social Action [BISA] VII, 6, in Rosales and Arévalo 1992, 230)

Dialogue as a "Manifestation of Lived Christianity"

From its earliest days, the FABC has chosen the quintessential Asian trait of *dialogue* as a "manifestation of lived Christianity" (Fernandes 1991, 548) to undergird its mission theology in response to the multicultural, multiethnic, and plurireligious challenges of the postcolonial Asian milieu, as well as the proximity of Asian Christians to their coreligionists. Dialogue is defined as "a process of talking and listening, of giving and receiving, of searching and studying, for the deepening and enriching of one another's faith and understanding" (Bishops' Institute for Interreligious Affairs [BIRA] I, 11, in Rosales and Arévalo 1992, 111). The foundation for the FABC's theology of dialogue is rooted in the Trinity:

> The basis of dialogue then is divine and trinitarian: the creative and salvific will of the Father, the cosmic outreach of the redemptive action of Jesus who is the Christ, and the recreative and fulfilling mystery of the Spirit. Dialogue is historical: it is the progressive unification of all things, that is at once the action of God in history and the free cooperation of peoples in building their own future. Dialogue is human: it is the expression in community of the common pilgrimage of peoples towards fulfillment. Dialogue is ecclesial: it is the very being and life of the Church as mission. (*Theses on Interreligious Dialogue*, 3.3, in FABC Office of Theological Concerns 1987, 9)

In its *Theses on Interreligious Dialogue*, the FABC Office of Theological Concerns lists out the goals of dialogue as follows: "mutual understanding, that dispels prejudices and promotes mutual knowledge and appreciation; mutual enrichment, that seeks to integrate into oneself values and experiences that are characteristic of and better developed by other believers for cultural, historical or providential reasons; common commitment to witness to and to promote human and spiritual values, like peace, respect for human life, human dignity, equality and freedom, justice, community and religious liberty, through awareness raising, prayer and action programs; shared religious experience, that constantly reaches out, in a deeper way, to the ultimate" (4.3, in FABC Office of Theological Concerns 1987, 10–11).

For the FABC, the goals of dialogue are "to promote mutual understanding and harmony" (BIRA I, 15, in Rosales and Arévalo 1992, 111), "to promote whatever leads to unity, love, truth, justice and peace" (BIRA I, 16, in Rosales and Arévalo 1992, 111) and to share "the riches of our spiritual heritages" (BIRA I, 17, in Rosales and Arévalo 1992, 111). For the FABC, dialogue is "not the search for the least common denominator, accompanied by an attempt to ignore whatever may provoke disagreement," but demands loyalty to one's own faith experience in a manner that confers a twofold benefit: "Exposure to the experience of others has a way of clarifying one's own experience and of deepening it. Trying to explain to another believer one's own belief is also one good way of clarifying to oneself what one believes. In this way, dialogue would lead to mutual enrichment rather than mutual impoverishment" (*Theses on Interreligious Dialogue*, 5.2, in FABC Office of Theological Concerns 1987, 12). Dialogue is also perceived as a process that "will normally start with tolerance and peaceful coexistence" before moving on to "a dialogue of life, promoting mutual acceptance and even admiration" (*Theses on Interreligious Dialogue*, 5.3, in FABC Office of Theological Concerns 1987, 12).

Dialogue with Asian Cultures, Religions, and the Poor

At their first gathering on November 29, 1960, the Asian Bishops' Meeting (ABM) passed a resolution to engage in "an open, sincere, and continuing dialogue with our brothers of other great religions of Asia, that we may learn from one another how to enrich ourselves spiritually and how to work more effectively together on our common task of total human development" (ABM, resolution 12, in Rosales and Arévalo 1992, 9). Four years later, the first FABC Plenary Assembly developed this nascent understanding of dialogue into a call for an intersectional *threefold dialogue* that comprises mutually respectful and critical encounters and interactions between Asian Christians and the subaltern Asian masses with their rich, diverse, and pluralistic cultures, religions, and experiences of poverty and marginalization (FABC I, 12 and 19, in Rosales and Arévalo 1992, 14–15). This call for an intersectional threefold dialogue has been emphasized by subsequent FABC statements, especially the fifth FABC Plenary Assembly (see FABC V, 3.1.2, in Rosales and Arévalo 1992, 280) and the sixth FABC Plenary Assembly (see FABC VI, 3, in Eilers 1997, 2). According to the FABC, this dialogue is to be carried out as *equal partners* with the Asian cultures, religions, and poor: "We enter as equal partners into the dialogue in a mutuality of sharing and enrichment contributing to mutual growth. It excludes any sense of competition. Rather, it centers on each other's values. All the partners in dialogue participate in their own culture, history and time. Hence, dialogue brings the partners more deeply into their own cultures and bears the characteristics of inculturation" (BIRA I, 12, in Rosales and Arévalo 1992, 111).

From the beginning, the Asian Catholic bishops have gone beyond their episcopal counterparts elsewhere in the world by their innovative and original theological position that the task of doing Christian mission in postcolonial Asia has to take place within this threefold dialogue in a spirit of goodwill. We see this as early as 1974 in the final statement of the first FABC Plenary Assembly, which insists that at the heart of the task of mission of the Asian local church lies the dialogical encounter between the local church and the Asian milieu, with its threefold reality of Asian cultures, religions, and poverty (see FABC I, 12, in Rosales and Arévalo 1992, 14).

The first FABC Plenary Assembly further clarifies that this "dialogue of life" requires "working, not for them merely (in a paternalistic sense), but *with* them, to learn from them" their "real needs and aspirations" and to "strive for their fulfillment" (FABC I, 20, in Rosales and Arévalo 1992, 15). Commenting on this theological innovation by the first FABC Plenary Assembly, Michael Amaladoss concludes that the FABC saw mission as dialogue with "the threefold realities of Asia"—that is, "its rich cultures, its ancient and great religions, and the poor"—because the Asian Catholic bishops accepted Asian religions as "significant and positive elements in the economy of God's design of salvation" in postcolonial Asia as a result of having "*a living experience of other religions*" (1991, 362; emphasis added).

Dialogue with Asian Cultures

The FABC's earliest reference to the categories of "culture" and "inculturation" is found in the final statement of the groundbreaking ABM of November 29, 1970:

> In the inculturation of the life and message of the Gospel in Asia, there have been hesitations and mistakes in the past, but we are more than ever convinced that dialogue with our fellow Asians whose commitment is to other faiths is increasingly important. We also urge on all a deep respect

for the culture and traditions of our peoples, and express the hope that the catholicity of the Church, the root of our diversity in the oneness of faith, may serve to help Asians remain truly Asian, and yet become fully part of the modern world and the one human family. (ABM 24, in Rosales and Arévalo 1992, 6)

Even at this early stage, the Asian Catholic bishops argue for a close connection between inculturation, interreligious dialogue, and respect for Asian cultures and traditions as the expression of the catholicity of the postcolonial Asian church. This powerful statement on inculturation in 1970 also reflects the Asian Catholic bishops' acknowledgment and deep understanding of postcolonial Asia's multifaceted diversity and plurality, recognizing "the face of Asia that is the continent of ancient and diverse cultures, religions, histories and traditions, a region like Joseph's coat of many colors" (ABM 7, in Rosales and Arévalo 1992, 4).

Subsequently, the Asian Catholic bishops unpack this incipient insight at their inaugural Plenary Assembly in 1974. The final statement of the first FABC Plenary Assembly links inculturation with the local Asian church in a dialogical encounter with every aspect of Asian lived realities:

The local Church is a Church incarnate in a people, a Church indigenous and inculturated. And this means concretely a Church in continuous, humble and loving dialogue with the living traditions, the cultures, the religions—in brief, with all the life-realities of the people in whose midst it has sunk its roots deeply and whose history and life it gladly makes its own. It seeks to share in whatever truly belongs to that people: its meanings and its values, its aspirations, its thoughts and its language, its songs and its artistry.— Even its frailties and failings it assumes, so that they too may be healed. For so did God's Son assume the totality of our fallen human condition (save only for sin) so that He might make it truly His own, and redeem it in His paschal mystery. (FABC I, 12, in Rosales and Arévalo 1992, 14)

Implicit in such a theological vision is the acknowledgment and acceptance of a fundamental ontological, soteriological, and existential relationship between the Christian gospel and the Asian peoples, with their rich religious and cultural traditions as well as their daily socioeconomic challenges.

For the FABC, this dialogical encounter "facilitates the incarnation of the Good News in the various cultures creating new ways of life, action, worship and reflection, so as to help the growth of the local Churches and to realize the catholicity and fullness of the mystery of Christ" (BIRA III, 5, in Rosales and Arévalo 1992, 120). More importantly, the Asian Catholic bishops view dialogue and inculturation as inextricably linked. For example, BIRA IV/1 insists, "We perceive dialogue as a necessary condition and instrument for inculturation" (BIRA IV/1, 12, in Rosales and Arévalo 1992, 249). In other words, inculturation exists neither on its own nor for its own sake but within an intersectional and interactive framework with interreligious dialogue in postcolonial Asia.

The final statement of the FABC Consultation on Christian Presence among Muslims in Asia (CCPMA) condemns any misapprehension of inculturation as a tactic to "convert people" to Christianity: "Inculturation like dialogue is not a tactic to convert people to one's faith. It lies at the very core of Christian incarnational faith, life and witness. It is the existential way a Christian lives and witnesses to his faith in the concrete religious, social and cultural milieu in which providence places him. Genuine inculturation takes place when Christians live out as individuals and as a community their double heritage of faith and country. This can come about only through inter-cultural and inter-religious dialogue" (CCPMA, art 31, in Rosales and Arévalo 1992, 170).

The FABC Theological Consultation, which met in Hua Hin, Thailand, in 1991, addresses the question of the theological foundations of inculturation in postcolonial Asia by giving it a christological and paschal orientation:

> The same conformity of the Church to her Master is the decisive theological foundation for the inculturation of local Churches. The Son of God became man in Jesus in a particular place at a particular time of history, two thousand years ago in Palestine. Jesus was a Jew, deeply inserted in the culture of his people. The revelation he conveyed of the mystery of God as well as the way in which he accomplished his messianic and saving mission are steeped in the religious tradition of Israel, even while they fulfill it in an unforeseen manner. The mystery of the Incarnation and the paschal mystery are at once the foundation and the model for the deep insertion of local Churches in the surrounding cultures, in all aspects of their life, celebration, witness and mission. (Theological Consultation, 35, in Rosales and Arévalo 1992, 343)

By far, the FABC's most thorough exposition of inculturation is to be found in the groundbreaking document *Theses on the Local Church: A Theological Reflection in the Asian Context* from the FABC's Office of Theological Concerns. *Theses on the Local Church* begins by stating the relationship between inculturation and the local church in postcolonial Asia as follows:

> A local Church comes into existence and is built up through a deep and mutually enriching encounter between the Gospel and a people with its particular culture and

tradition. In current theological and magisterial language, this is known as inculturation. Inculturation consists not only in the expression of the Gospel and the Christian faith through the cultural medium, but includes, as well, experiencing, understanding and appropriating them through the cultural resources of a people. As a result, the concrete shape of the local Church will be, on the one hand, conditioned by the culture, and on the other hand, the culture will be evangelized by the life and witness of the local Church. (thesis 5, in FABC Office of Theological Concerns 1991, 18)

According to *Theses on the Local Church*, inculturation is the "attempt to contextualize the life and mission of the Church by bringing faith and culture into closer relationship" (5.01, in FABC Office of Theological Concerns 1991, 18). It is grounded in an *encounter* of "mutuality and reciprocity" between the Christian gospel and Asian cultures (5.02, 5.04, in FABC Office of Theological Concerns 1991, 19, 20). The rationale for inculturation of local churches engaging in a dialogue with cultures is explained by *Theses on the Local Church* as follows: "Each culture not only provides us with a new approach to the human, but also opens up new avenues for the understanding of the Gospel and its riches. When the Gospel encounters the tradition, experience and culture of a people, its hitherto undiscovered virtualities will surface; riches and meanings as yet hidden will emerge into the light. That is why it is so important to reinterpret the Gospel through the cultural resources of every people; this reinterpretation truly enriches the Christian tradition" (5.07, in FABC Office of Theological Concerns 1991, 20–21).

At the same time, *Theses on the Local Church* warns against any simplistic understanding of culture in instrumentalizing terms:

It should be clear that culture, which has its basis in God's creation of man and nature, should be respected in its inner purpose and goal and should not be viewed simply as a means for something else. Nor should individual elements of culture be isolated from the organic whole. Hence, inculturation cannot be a process in which particular elements of a culture are selected to serve as a garb for the Gospel. This will be a very external and superficial kind of inculturation since it does not respect the inner soul of the culture and its organic character. (5.06, in FABC Office of Theological Concerns 1991, 20)

On the one hand, *Theses on the Local Church* asserts the necessity for the Christian gospel to be "experienced and understood through the cultural resources of a people" because, "given the historicity of human existence in a determined context and tradition, it is inescapable that our perception of truth, understanding and experiencing of reality—including the Gospel and faith—be bound up with a particular culture" (5.08, in FABC Office of Theological Concerns 1991, 21). On the other hand, *Theses on the Local Church* also insists on the need for the Christian gospel to effect a prophetic critique of the Asian cultures because "Asian cultures are ambiguous, in the sense that, along with many lofty ideals, visions and values, they contain also oppressive and anti-human elements, such as caste, which goes against the equality of all human beings, discrimination towards women, etc." (6.08, in FABC Office of Theological Concerns 1991, 25). Hence *Theses on the Local Church* declares that "it is not enough to say that culture conditions the shape of the local Church. In the same breath we should also add that the Gospel too acts on culture" (5.12, in FABC Office of Theological Concerns 1991, 22).

Theses on the Local Church also makes three significant contributions to the discussion on inculturation. First, it highlights the need for inculturation to promote harmony:

The encounter of the Gospel need not always be with one
homogeneous culture. It could be with a diversity of ethnic,
linguistic or cultural groups living in the same locality. In
fact, in some countries in Asia we have in the same local
Church the presence of various ethnic and cultural groups.
This mosaic of various languages, cultures and peoples
is a great enrichment for the local Church. The process
of inculturation must take into account this concrete
situation as well as the evolution and growth, which
these diverse human groups undergo as part of a region
or nation. In situations of conflict of ethnic or cultural
identities, the local Church can serve as an agent of unity
and reconciliation. It will foster the communion of various
cultures and traditions and thereby shape its own specific
identity as a local Church. *In multi-racial, multi-linguistic
and pluri-cultural situations the task of inculturation
would involve also the promotion of harmony and
communion.* (5.11, in FABC Office of Theological Concerns
1991, 22; emphasis added)

Second, *Theses on the Local Church* expands on the earlier
christological and paschal dimensions of inculturation in the FABC
Theological Consultation of 1991 to include the role of the Holy
Spirit at Pentecost in the process of inculturation, pointing out
that "a local Church realizes itself through a process of inculturation by following the dynamic of Incarnation, the Paschal Mystery
and Pentecost" (thesis 10, in FABC Office of Theological Concerns
1991, 33). *Theses on the Local Church* explains the rationale for this
threefold dynamic of inculturation as follows:

The miracle of the Pentecost (Acts 2) provides biblical
grounding for the task of inculturation. Pentecost
manifests the Church's unity in the midst of diversity,

which is Catholic fullness (*catholica unitas*). It grounds the authentic catholicity of the Church in the creative power of the Spirit. The Spirit alone enables the Church to be one amidst the diversity of peoples and races and amidst the multiplicity of human situations. For the mystery of the Church's catholicity, as it is actualized in history, is ultimately rooted in the presence and action of the Spirit. Human efforts to create a universal communion without God end up either in the monolithic uniformity of the Tower of Babel (Gen 11:1–9) or a chaotic heterogeneity and individualism to which history attests. Only in the power of the Word and the Spirit can a world of true human communion be built up on our planet, bringing to fulfillment and fruition all the richness of human cultures and their realizations. (10.10, in FABC Office of Theological Concerns 1991, 35)

Third, *Theses on the Local Church* makes a brief but highly significant reference to the need for liturgical inculturation:

A very important area of inculturation is the liturgy of the Christian community. Liturgy expresses the faith of the Church (*lex orandi lex credendi*). Liturgy must be the outcome of the faith-experience in a particular cultural environment. In turn, such liturgical experience should flower in a Christian life that is fully inculturated. Therefore, true liturgical inculturation of the Christian community cannot be done from without and introduced through an external and artificial process; it should spontaneously spring forth from the life of the faith lived fully in the context of the culture and the life-realities of the people. Nevertheless, given the long estrangement of the liturgical life of Asian local Churches from their cultural traditions, at this stage of transition to a fully inculturated ecclesial life, certain liturgical experiments and models are very legitimate and necessary in order to facilitate the process of inculturation by the whole community. These experiments, however, should not reflect only the concerns of a few experts, but rather should be in dialogue with the whole Christian community. (8.03, in FABC Office of Theological Concerns 1991, 28–29)

Theses on the Local Church follows this up with further recommendations in the section entitled "Pastoral Corollaries and Recommendations": "We recommend more leeway be given in inculturating the liturgy. Responsible experiments in the liturgy with 'control groups,' accompanied and fostered by due catechesis, should be encouraged so that new inculturated liturgical expressions may be discovered and developed. We urge the Episcopal Conferences eventually to approve and present for general use among their faithful some diverse inculturated liturgical expressions" (V, 1 and 2, in FABC Office of Theological Concerns 1991, 55–56).

From all of these FABC documents, we see that from the very beginning, the FABC recognizes that inculturation is more than merely a superficial external adaptation of Christian beliefs, structures, and practices to the postcolonial Asian reality. In the panorama of cultural diversity and religious pluralism in postcolonial Asia, the FABC understands inculturation to be a *dialogical encounter* between the gospel and the local church within the postcolonial Asian reality as an intersectional and integrated whole of Asian cultures, religions, and the subaltern Asian masses of the poor and marginalized. Here we see that Christianity not only enriches but also in turn is enriched by the postcolonial Asian cultural, religious, and social realities. Without this mutual relationship, inculturation runs the risk of cultural appropriation and instrumentalization—that is to say, appropriating elements of Asian sociocultural and religious realities for Christian use without respecting their integrity within their own contexts.

More significantly, the FABC's holistic understanding of inculturation also reveals a preferential option for Asian cultures, spirituality, and religiosity in recognition of the fact that the postcolonial Asian milieu is defined by intersectional dimensions of diverse cultures and plurireligiosity, as well as intense poverty and marginalization among the subaltern Asian peoples. Thus the FABC's integrative approach to inculturation enables it to respond credibly and effectively to the "signs of the times" in postcolonial Asia. In short, the FABC views inculturation as more than merely a pastoral issue or methodology. Rather, inculturation is an existential quest of "immersing" the local Asian churches and faith communities in the diverse and pluralistic postcolonial Asian milieu, with its myriad cultures, religions, and extreme poverty and marginalization, sharing life in solidarity with the Asian peoples and serving life as Jesus has done (FABC VI, 14.2, in Eilers 1997, 8).

Dialogue with Asian Religions

As is the case with dialogue with Asian cultures, the 1970 ABM also insists on the importance of engaging in a dialogue with the Asian religions: "We pledge ourselves to an open, sincere, and continuing dialogue with our brothers of other great religions of Asia, that we may learn from one another how to enrich ourselves spiritually and how to work more effectively together on our common task of total human development" (resolution 12, in Rosales and Arévalo 1992, 9). In giving a privileged place to the many religious traditions of the Asian peoples, the first FABC Plenary Assembly is unequivocal on the need for seeing Asian religions as "significant and positive elements in the economy of God's design of salvation":

In this dialogue we accept them [i.e., the great religious traditions of Asia] as significant and positive elements in the economy of God's design of salvation. In them we recognize and respect profound spiritual and ethical meanings and values. Over many centuries they have been the treasuries of the religious experience of our ancestors, from which our contemporaries do not cease to draw light and strength. They have been (and continue to be) the authentic expression of the noblest longings of their hearts, and the home of their contemplation and prayer. They have helped to give shape to the histories and cultures of our nations. (FABC I, 14, in Rosales and Arévalo 1992, 14)

FABC I also stresses that it is only through dialogue that the Asian local churches are able to give due reverence and honor to these Asian religions and acknowledge that God has drawn these religions to Godself (FABC I, 15, in Rosales and Arévalo 1992, 14).

More importantly, the FABC also affirms that "it is an inescapable truth that God's Spirit is at work in all religious traditions" (BIRA IV/12, 7, in Rosales and Arévalo 1992, 326) because "it has been recognized since the time of the apostolic Church, and stated clearly again by the Second Vatican Council, that the Spirit of Christ is active outside the bounds of the visible Church" (BIRA II, 12, in Rosales and Arévalo 1992, 115). Hence interreligious dialogue "is based on the firm belief that the Holy Spirit is operative in other religions as well" (BIRA IV/2, 8.5, in Rosales and Arévalo 1992, 253) because the religious traditions of Asia "are expressions of the presence of God's Word and of the universal action of his Spirit in them" (Theological Consultation, 43, in Rosales and Arévalo 1992, 344). In particular, the "great religions of Asia with their respective creeds, cults and codes reveal to us diverse ways of responding to God whose Spirit is active in all peoples and cultures" (BIRA IV/7, 12, in Rosales and Arévalo 1992, 310). For the FABC, it is "the same

spirit, who has been active in the incarnation, life, death and resurrection of Jesus and in the Church, who was active among all
peoples before the Incarnation and is active among the nations,
religions and peoples of Asia today" (BIRA IV/3, 6, in Rosales and
Arévalo 1992, 259).

Dialogue with the Asian Poor

The first FABC Plenary Assembly is adamant that Asian Christians have to participate in a "dialogue of life" with the poor that
involves a genuine experience and understanding of the poverty,
deprivation, and oppression of the subaltern Asian peoples (FABC
I, 20, in Rosales and Arévalo 1992, 15). In this discussion, the FABC
understands the category of "poor" in a dialectical sense: "Poor,
not in human values, qualities, nor in human potential. But poor,
in that they are deprived of access to material goods and resources
which they need to create a truly human life for themselves.
Deprived, because they live under oppression, that is, under social,
economic and political structures which have injustice built into
them" (FABC I, 19, in Rosales and Arévalo 1992, 15).

In turn, this gives rise to a genuine commitment and effort
to bring about social justice in postcolonial Asia (FABC I, 21, in
Rosales and Arévalo 1992, 15). In so doing, the FABC I unequivocally
affirms the statement of the 1971 Special Synod of Bishops, *Justice
in the World*, which declares that "actions on behalf of justice and
participation in the transformation of the world fully appear to us
as a constitutive dimension of preaching of the Gospel . . . , for we
believe that this, in our time, is part and parcel of 'preaching the
Good News to the poor'" (FABC I, 22, in Rosales and Arévalo 1992,
15–16). FABC I also underscores the connection between evangelization, human development, and liberation: "Evangelization and
the promotion of true human development and liberation, are not
only not opposed, but make up today the integral preaching of

the Gospel, especially in Asia" (FABC I, 23, in Rosales and Arévalo 1992, 16). As far as the FABC is concerned, the poor are seen as "ultimately the privileged community and agents of salvation (as has always been the case in the history of salvation)" (International Congress on Mission, 4, in Rosales and Arévalo 1992, 144). Using a powerful metaphor of pitching tents among the subaltern Asian masses, the sixth FABC Plenary Assembly explains, "Like Jesus, we 'have to pitch our tents' in the midst of all humanity building a better world, but especially among the suffering and the poor, the marginalized and the downtrodden of Asia. In profound 'solidarity with suffering humanity' and led by the Spirit of life, we need to immerse ourselves in Asia's cultures of poverty and deprivation, from whose depths the aspirations for love and life are most poignant and compelling. Serving life demands communion with every woman and man seeking and struggling for life, in the way of Jesus' solidarity with humanity" (FABC VI, 14.2, in Eilers 1997, 8).

Mission as Threefold Dialogue

The FABC is insistent that dialogue is "an integral part of evangelization" (Bishops' Institute for Missionary Apostolate [BIMA] II, 14, in Rosales and Arévalo 1992, 100), "intrinsic to the very life of the Church" (BIRA I, 9, in Rosales and Arévalo 1992, 111), and an "essential mode of all evangelization" (International Congress on Mission, 19, in Rosales and Arévalo 1992, 131). The third consensus paper that was presented at the FABC International Congress on Mission speaks of dialogue as bringing "to the local churches in Asia which are in danger of being ghettos an openness to and integration into the mainstream of their cultures. Christians grow in genuine love for their neighbors of other faiths, and the latter learn to love their Christian neighbors" (4b, in Rosales and Arévalo 1992, 142). In the context of the cultural diversity and religious pluralism of postcolonial Asia, the FABC sees dialogue as leading to *"receptive pluralism,* that is, the many ways of responding to the promptings of the Holy Spirit must be continually in conversation with one another" (BIRA IV/3, 16, in Rosales and Arévalo 1992, 261).

It is the overarching vision of the FABC that "the Church is called to be a community of dialogue. This dialogical model is in fact a new way of being Church" (BIRA IV/12, 48, in Rosales and Arévalo 1992, 332). The FABC perceives that the Asian church "is never centered on itself but on the coming true of God's dream for the world. It seeks not to exclude others but to be truly catholic in its concerns, in its appreciation of the gifts of others, and in its readiness to work with others for a world at once more human and more divine" (BIRA IV/12, 49, in Rosales and Arévalo 1992, 333). Building on the incipient insights of the first FABC Plenary Assembly, the Asian bishops have subsequently accepted inter-religious dialogue as a constitutive element of being church in postcolonial Asia: "Interreligious dialogue flows from the nature of the Church, a community in pilgrimage journeying with peoples of other faiths towards the Kingdom that is to come" (BIRA IV/4, 2, in Rosales and Arévalo 1992, 300).

Such a deep and profound theology of mission enables the postcolonial Asian church to move away from "an institution planted in Asia" toward "an evangelizing community of Asia" (Theological Consultation, 15, in Rosales and Arévalo 1992, 338). Clearly, the FABC has great hopes that the local church is able to be deeply inculturated in the Asian soil to the extent that it becomes not simply a church in Asia but truly a postcolonial Asian church (BIRA IV/12, 50, in Rosales and Arévalo 1992, 333).

Proclamation through Dialogue

As far as the FABC is concerned, "religious dialogue is not just a substitute for or a mere preliminary to the proclamation of Christ, but should be the ideal form of evangelization, where in humility and mutual support we seek together with our brothers and sisters that fullness of Christ which is God's plan for the whole of creation, in its entirety and its great and wonderful diversity" (BIMA I, 10, in Rosales and Arévalo 1992, 94). On the one hand, this call for dialogue does not mean that the FABC has abandoned the task of proclaiming the Christian gospel in postcolonial Asia. In its groundbreaking document *Theses on Interreligious Dialogue* (1987), the FABC Office of Theological Concerns seeks to clarify the relationship between dialogue and proclamation in the task of Christian mission in postcolonial Asia. Of the seven theses enunciated in the document, thesis 6 asserts, "Dialogue and proclamation are integral but dialectical and complementary dimensions of the Church's mission of evangelization. Authentic dialogue includes a witness to one's total Christian faith, which is open to a similar witness of the other religious believers. Proclamation is a call to Christian discipleship and mission. As a service to the mystery of the Spirit who freely calls to conversion, and of the person who freely responds to the call, proclamation is dialogical" (in FABC Office of Theological Concerns 1987, 15). As the *Theses on Interreligious Dialogue* unpacks this statement, it warns against any facile reduction of one to the other:

> The relation between dialogue and proclamation is a complex one. In making an effort to understand this relationship, we must avoid from the beginning any attempt to reduce one to the other. Some would tend to say that dialogue itself is the only authentic form of proclamation since the Church is only one among the many ways to salvation; others would tend to say that dialogue is only a step, though with an identity of its own, in the total process that culminates in proclamation. While the former approach robs proclamation of any specific meaning, the

latter instrumentalizes dialogue. (6.2, in FABC Office of
Theological Concerns 1987, 15)

Theses on Interreligious Dialogue stresses that rather than being
construed in abstract terms, proclamation should be understood
within the context of and integrated into the FABC's theology of
threefold dialogue with Asian cultures, religions, and the poor:
"The Asian bishops have understood evangelization as the building up of the local church through a threefold dialogue with the
cultures, the religions and the poor of Asia. Inculturation, interreligious dialogue and liberation are the three dimensions of evangelization. Proclamation is not a fourth dimension added to these
three, but is the aspect of witness that is an integral element of
all the three dimensions of evangelization" (6.4, in FABC Office
of Theological Concerns 1987, 16).

On the other hand, the FABC makes it clear that it does not
exclude the explicit verbal proclamation of the Christian gospel
as mission while at the same time recognizing that context plays
an important role in determining the best approach to mission. In
this regard, the fifth FABC Plenary Assembly explains that dialogue
does not preclude the need for the proclamation of the Christian
gospel. FABC V points out that there could be a moment when
"we shall not be timid when God opens the door for us to *proclaim*
explicitly the Lord Jesus Christ as the Savior and the answer to
the fundamental questions of human existence" (FABC V, 4.3, in
Rosales and Arévalo 1992, 282). However, FABC V also states that
a distinctively Asian approach of proclamation that is sensitive to
the realities of postcolonial Asia is needed:

Mission may find its greatest urgency in Asia; it also finds
in our continent a distinctive mode. We affirm, together
with others, that "the proclamation of Jesus Christ is the
center and primary element of evangelization" (Statement

of the FABC All-Asia Conference on Evangelization, Suwon, South Korea, August 24–31, 1988). But the proclamation of Jesus Christ in Asia means, first of all, the witness of Christians and of Christian communities to the values of the Kingdom of God, *a proclamation through Christlike deeds.* For Christians in Asia, to proclaim Christ means above all to live like him, in the midst of our neighbors of other faiths and persuasions, and to do his deeds by the power of his grace. Proclamation through dialogue and deeds—this is the first call to the Churches in Asia. (FABC V, 4.1, in Rosales and Arévalo 1992, 281–82)

More importantly, FABC V unequivocally links the task of doing Christian mission in postcolonial Asia with the call to engage in a threefold dialogue with Asia's cultures, religious traditions, and poor: "Mission includes: being with the people, responding to their needs, with sensitiveness to the presence of God in cultures and other religious traditions, and witnessing to the values of God's Kingdom through presence, solidarity, sharing and word. *Mission will mean a dialogue with Asia's poor, with its local cultures, and with other religious traditions*" (FABC V, 3.1.2, in Rosales and Arévalo 1992, 280; emphasis added). In this paradigm shift in understanding mission as dialogue, we see how FABC V builds on an important insight in the final statement of the third BIMA meeting in Changhua, Taiwan, in 1982:

It is true that in many places [in Asia] Christ cannot yet be proclaimed openly by words. But He can, and should be, proclaimed through other ways, namely: through the witness of life of the Christian community and family, and their striving to know and live more fully the faith they possess; through their desire to live in peace and harmony with those who do not share our faith; through the appreciation by Christians of the human and religious values possessed by their non-Christian neighbors, and through these same Christians' willingness to collaborate in those activities which promote the human community. (BIMA III, 10, in Rosales and Arévalo 1992, 105)

One of the inherent dangers of proclamation is that it often comes across as being overly discursive and defensive—that is, there is an abundance of words in proclamation that seek to prove or emphasize specific truth claims in debates with other religious adherents in a zero-sum game. By contrast, Felix Wilfred has pointed out that in the Asian mindset, "truth does not impose itself, but rather *attracts* everyone and everything to itself by its beauty, splendour and fascination" (1988, 427).

As for the relationship between dialogue, proclamation, and conversion, the FABC insists that "dialogue and proclamation are complementary. Sincere and authentic dialogue does not have for its objective the conversion of the other. For conversion depends solely on God's internal call and the person's free decision" (BIRA III, 4, in Rosales and Arévalo 1992, 120). Elsewhere, the FABC reiterates that "dialogue aimed at 'converting' the other to one's own religious faith and tradition is dishonest and unethical; it is not the way of harmony" (BIRA V/3, 7, in Eilers 1997, 158). On this issue, the late Angelo Fernandes, archbishop emeritus of Delhi, in his keynote address at BIRA IV/12 in February 1991, contends that Asians of other faiths ought to be regarded not as "objects of Christian mission" but as "partners in the Asian community, where there must be mutual witness" (1991, 548). Archbishop Fernandes explains that the dialogue between the Asian church and the Asian peoples should be seen as a "manifestation of lived Christianity" with its own integrity that leads toward the Reign of God (548).

Through a threefold dialogue with Asian cultures, religions, and the subaltern Asian poor and marginalized, the FABC recognizes that its missional endeavors could not only enrich but also be enriched by the sociocultural realities of postcolonial Asia. At the same time, the FABC stresses the importance of using methods and approaches that are indigenous to postcolonial Asia when it emphasizes that dialogue and missional outreach ought to "be truly Asian, employing the procedures for arriving at consensus for action which our people have themselves elaborated, rather than alien techniques which may work well enough in other cultures, but not in our own" (BISA I, 9, in Rosales and Arévalo 1992, 200). Commenting, Michael Amaladoss observes that doing Christian mission as a threefold dialogue with the cultural, religious, and subaltern realities of postcolonial Asia "means that we do not import readymade structures of 'salvation' from somewhere, but we let the people of Asia dialogue with the Good News in a creative and relevant way" (2000, 340).

At the same time, the fifth FABC Plenary Assembly underscores the close nexus between the task of doing mission, engaging in dialogue, responding to the challenges of conflicts and division, and the postcolonial Asian church as a "visible sign and instrument of unity and harmony": "Mission in Asia will also seek through *dialogue* to serve the cause of unity of the peoples of Asia marked by such a diversity of beliefs, cultures and socio-political structures. In an Asia marked by diversity and torn by conflicts, the Church must in a special way be a sacrament—a visible sign and instrument of unity and harmony" (FABC V, 4.2, in Rosales and Arévalo 1992, 282). Here we find the FABC—in recognizing the importance of mission as dialogue and calling for the Asian church to be a sacrament of unity and harmony in postcolonial Asia—is making an especially prophetic and powerful theological statement in response to the challenges of ongoing religious strife, racial-ethnic violence, and political conflicts that have devastated many parts of contemporary Asia, as we read in chapter 1. Clearly, proclamation without dialogue runs the risk of aggressive proselytism, which plays right into the hands of religious fundamentalists and zealots who are looking for convenient excuses to crack down on Asian Christians. As far as the FABC is concerned, the postcolonial Asian church will have "to discern, in dialogue with Asian peoples and Asian realities, what deeds the Lord wills to be done so that all humankind may be gathered together in harmony as his family" (FABC V, 6.3, in Rosales and Arévalo 1992, 283).

Ushering in the Reign of God in Postcolonial Asia

The FABC's regnocentric vision of doing Christian mission in postcolonial Asia is "rooted in the conviction of faith that God's plan of salvation for humanity is one and reaches out to all peoples: it is the Kingdom of God through which he seeks to reconcile all things with himself in Jesus Christ" (*Theses on Interreligious Dialogue*, 2.3, in FABC Office of Theological Concerns 1987, 7). As the document *Theses on Interreligious Dialogue* puts it, "The focus of the Church's mission of evangelization is building up the Kingdom of God and building up the Church to be at the service of the Kingdom. The Kingdom of God is therefore wider than the Church. The Church is the sacrament of the Kingdom, visibilizing it, ordained to it, promoting it, but not equating itself with it" (6.3, in FABC Office of Theological Concerns 1987, 16).

A year later, that statement is affirmed at the 1988 FABC All-Asia Conference on Evangelization, which explains that the "ultimate goal of all evangelization is the ushering in and establishment of God's Kingdom, namely God's rule in the hearts and minds of our people" (BIMA IV, 5, in Rosales and Arévalo 1992, 292). More importantly, the FABC clarifies the relationship between the church and the Reign of God as follows: "*The Reign of God is the very reason for the being of the Church*. The Church exists in and for the Kingdom. The Kingdom, God's gift and initiative, is already begun and is continually being realized, and made present through the Spirit. Where God is accepted, when the Gospel values are lived, where man is respected . . . there is the Kingdom. *It is far wider than the Church's boundaries.* This already present reality is oriented toward the final manifestation and full perfection of the Reign of God" (BIRA IV/2, 8.1, in Rosales and Arévalo 1992, 252; emphasis added).

Along the same lines, the FABC Theological Consultation of 1991 insists,

> The Reign of God is a universal reality, extending far beyond the boundaries of the Church. It is the reality of salvation in Jesus Christ, in which Christians and others share together. It is the fundamental "mystery of unity" which unites us more deeply than differences in religious allegiance are able to keep us apart. Seen in this manner, a "regnocentric" approach to mission theology does not in any way threaten the Christo-centric perspective of our faith. On the contrary, "regno-centrism" calls for "christo-centrism," and vice-versa, for it is in Jesus Christ and through the Christ-event that God has established his Kingdom upon the earth and in human history. (30, in Rosales and Arévalo 1992, 342)

Hence Lorenzo Fernando is able to conclude that as far as the FABC is concerned, the "Kingdom of God is neither identified with the Church nor restricted to particular religions but is within and beyond all religions. It is the Kingdom that becomes the meeting point of all religions" (2000, 867).

In other words, the FABC's regnocentric theology of mission is based on a positive understanding of the diversity and pluralism of postcolonial Asia, recognizing the grace and presence of God in all of creation in a mysterious manner (FABC I, 15, in Rosales and Arévalo

1992, 14; BIRA III, 2, in Rosales and Arévalo 1992, 119). The FABC sees the Asian church as "constantly moving forward in mission, as it accompanies all humankind in its pilgrimage to the Kingdom of the Father" (FABC III, 15, in Rosales and Arévalo 1992, 60). In addition, the 1991 FABC Theological Consultation states, "If the Church is the sacrament of the Kingdom, the reason is that she is the sacrament of Jesus Christ himself who is the mystery of salvation, to whom she is called to bear witness and whom she is called to announce. To be at the service of the Kingdom means for the Church to announce Jesus Christ" (33, in Rosales and Arévalo 1992, 342).

In making this point, the FABC is convinced that the divine plan of salvation is wider than the church and, more significantly, that the "church does not monopolize God's action in the universe," as the *Theses on Interreligious Dialogue* makes it clear:

The one divine plan of salvation for all peoples embraces the whole universe. The mission of the Church has to be understood within the context of this plan. *The Church does not monopolize God's action in the universe.* While it is aware of a special mission from God in the world, it *has to be attentive to God's action in the world*, as manifested also in the other religions. This twofold awareness constitutes the two poles of the Church's evangelizing action in relation to other religions. While proclamation is the expression of its awareness of being in mission, *dialogue is the expression of its awareness of God's presence and action outside its boundaries. . . .* Proclamation is the affirmation of and witness to God's action in oneself. Dialogue is the openness and attention to the mystery of God's action in the other believer. *It is a perspective of faith that we cannot speak of the one without the other.* (6.5, in FABC Office of Theological Concerns 1987, 16; emphasis added)

Theses on Interreligious Dialogue also maintains that the call to conversion and discipleship points primarily toward God and only secondarily toward the church: "The pilgrim Church witnesses not to itself but to the mystery; and calls to conversion and discipleship refer primarily to the relationship between God who calls and the person who responds. Only secondarily do they refer to the Church-community. The identity of the Church does not lie in being the exclusive 'ark of salvation' but in *being in mission to transform the world from within as leaven*, without being fully aware of the forms that such transformation may lead to" (6.12, in FABC Office of Theological Concerns 1987, 18; emphasis added).

As the FABC sees it, a regnocentric theology of mission in postcolonial Asia also challenges the Asian church to work "with the Christians of other Churches, together with our sisters and brothers of other faiths and with all people of goodwill, to make the Kingdom of God more visibly present in Asia" (FABC V, 2.3.9, in Rosales and Arévalo 1992, 279). Elsewhere in the same statement, the fifth FABC Plenary Assembly asserts that mission in postcolonial Asia seeks "to proclaim the Good News of the Kingdom of God: to promote the values of the Kingdom such as justice, peace, love, compassion, equality and brotherhood in these Asian realities" (1.7, in Rosales and Arévalo 1992, 275).

The inclusivity of the Reign of God holds great appeal to the FABC, which "acknowledges the Kingdom at work in socio-political situations and in cultural and religious traditions of Asia" (Theological Consultation, 39, in Rosales and Arévalo 1992, 344). As Felix Wilfred explains, the inclusive nature of the Reign of God is able to encompass those people who are inspired by Jesus Christ and his good news but choose for various reasons to remain within the religious traditions that they have grown up with:

We have in Asia the phenomenon of a lot of men and women who are gripped by Jesus, his life and teachings.

They are his devotees while they continue to be Hindus, Buddhists, Taoists. What is particularly remarkable is that they can be Hindus, or Buddhists, etc., and devotees of Christ without being syncretistic. Syncretism, they feel, is something which is attributed to them from the outside, while from within, at the level of their consciousness, they experience unity and harmony, and are not assailed by those contradictions and conflicts which may appear to those who look at them from without. (1988, 429)

In chapter 6, we will explore insider movements generally and the Khrist Bhaktas specifically as examples of followers of Jesus within a regnocentric soteriology while remaining institutionally outside of traditional ecclesial structures and membership.

Toward "Active Integral Evangelization"

At the beginning of the third Christian millennium, some thirty years after the Asian Catholic bishops gathered for the first time in Manila for Pope Paul VI's historic visit to Asia, the seventh Plenary Assembly of the FABC was convened on the theme of "A Renewed Church in Asia on a Mission of Love and Service." At this assembly, the FABC introduces a new theological paradigm, "active integral evangelization" (Eilers 2002, 3), to articulate a distinctively Asian approach to Christian mission that integrates the intersecting dimensions of commitment and service to the Asian peoples, life witness, threefold dialogue, and bringing about the Reign of God in the diverse and pluralistic postcolonial Asian world:

For thirty years, as we have tried to reformulate our Christian identity in Asia, we have addressed different issues, one after another: evangelization, inculturation, dialogue, the Asian-ness of the Church, justice, the option for the poor, etc. Today, after three decades, we no longer speak of such distinct issues. We are addressing present needs that are massive and increasingly complex. *These issues are not separate topics to be discussed, but aspects of an integrated approach to our Mission of Love and Service. We need to feel and act "integrally." As we face the needs of the 21st century, we do so with Asian hearts, in solidarity with the poor and the marginalized, in union with all our Christian brothers and sisters, and by joining hands with all men and women of Asia of many different faiths. Inculturation, dialogue, justice and the option for the poor are aspects of whatever we do.* (Eilers 2002, 8; emphasis added)

Within this pivotal moment in the history of the FABC, FABC VII reiterates an important theological point that was previously stated by FABC VI—the FABC is committed to the "emergence of the Asianness of the Church in Asia" that is "an embodiment of the Asian vision and values of life, especially interiority, harmony, a holistic and inclusive approach to every area of life" (Eilers 2002, 8). More significantly, FABC VII is convinced that this "Asianness of the Church in Asia" is "a special gift the world is awaiting" (9). As it explains, "The whole world is in need of a holistic paradigm for meeting the challenges of life," and "together with all Asians, the Church, a tiny minority in this vast continent, has a singular contribution to make, and this contribution is the task of the whole Church in Asia" (9). In addition, the FABC affirms that the "most effective means of evangelization and service in the name of Christ has always been and continues to be the *witness of life*" (12; emphasis added). This witness of life that flows from active integral evangelization is needed more than ever in response to the challenges posed by religious fundamentalists and exclusivists in many parts of Asia, which we previously discussed in chapter 1.

A Postcolonial Asian Mission Theology

The FABC's postcolonial mission theology begins not from above or from the center but from below and from the periphery, moving toward the center. For the FABC, the task of Christian mission in postcolonial Asia is not a one-way street, a unidirectional proclamation of abstract creedal principles, theological precepts, and doctrinal truths in competitive apologetical debates with the creedal principles and truths of other religions. In articulating its approach to the task of doing Christian mission in postcolonial Asia, the FABC begins not with abstract and universalistic theological concepts and categories but with the daily life experiences and challenges arising from the ongoing encounters with the subaltern Asian peoples, with their diversity and plurality of cultures, religions, and experiences of poverty and marginalization in postcolonial Asia. The FABC is mindful that they are called neither to conquer the postcolonial Asian world in the name of a triumphant Christ nor to establish a triumphant Christendom on Asian soil but rather to bring about an Asian Christian presence that is relational and dialogical instead of over and against Asian cultures and religions. More importantly, the FABC is adamant that religious pluralism lies at the heart of what it means to be Asian and Christian, perceiving the Asian church's mission in postcolonial Asia as inspired by God's *prior* activity in the world through the workings of the Holy Spirit in Asia. As far as the FABC is concerned, the deep soteriological underpinnings and sapiential orientation of Asian religions and cultures that have nourished the lives of the Asian peoples are divinely inspired by the Holy Spirit being active outside the boundaries of the institutional Church, a point that the FABC made as far back as the first FABC Plenary Assembly in 1974. Beyond dialogue and proclamation, the FABC also sees one of the tasks of doing Christian mission in Asia as working together with other Asian religions on the goal of ushering in the Reign of God in Asia.

The centerpiece of the FABC's mission theology is the quintessential Asian practice of dialogue that seeks to facilitate mutual and intersectional interactions between the Christian gospel and the threefold reality of Asian cultures, religions, and experiences of poverty and marginalization across postcolonial Asia. For the FABC, Christian mission is about not only the postcolonial Asian cultural, religious, and socioeconomic realities being transformed by Christianity but also Christianity being enriched by its encounter with these things. For the FABC, life witness and dialogue are two sides of the same coin that define the relationship between the Christian gospel and other religious traditions in the pluralistic Asian landscape, enabling Asian Christians to share the good news with their fellow Asians. Undoubtedly, the FABC regards dialogue as necessary to redress the damage that has been perpetrated by centuries of European imperialism and colonial domination in Asia. In particular, dialogue has the potential to bring about opportunities for two or more parties, with their different worldviews, to enter into each other's horizons in order to foster improved relations between them. While the sapiential Asian vision of the FABC does not neglect the importance of proclamation, it also values and stresses the importance of friendship and trust, relationality and relationship building, and dialogue and solidarity as foundational constitutive elements of doing Christian mission in Asia.

The FABC's preferred mode of mission as a threefold dialogue points to a missional praxis that seeks to be in solidarity, empathy, and collaboration with the Asian peoples. As far as the FABC is concerned, the focus of Christian mission in postcolonial Asia is regnocentric rather than ecclesiocentric. In this regard, the FABC has reiterated repeatedly that the task of Christian mission, although necessary, is to be done not for its own sake, or even for the sake of establishing new churches or promoting church growth, but to bring about the Reign of God among the peoples of postcolonial Asia. It is noteworthy that the FABC emphasizes the need to critique, transform, and heal the violence, hatred, and brokenness across postcolonial Asia in the name of ushering in the Reign of God. More importantly, in seeking to serve the Reign of God in Asia, the Asian church is called to contribute to Asian cultures, religions, and redressing socioeconomic challenges, even if these cultures, religions, and societies do not become institutionally Christian.

Hence the FABC's mission theology entails a commitment to work in harmony with the lived realities of postcolonial Asia. In this regard, the FABC points out that the Asian church is called to mission by bringing the life and hope of the good news of Jesus Christ to an Asia that is beset with challenges and problems. To be truly Asian and at home in the postcolonial Asian milieu, the church is challenged to embrace the cultural diversity, religious pluralism, and the marginalizing subaltern life experiences of postcolonial Asia while at the same time prophetically challenging and purifying their oppressive and life-denying elements in the name of the Christian gospel. In this regard, the FABC perceives the task of Christian mission as working for the redemption of humanity in postcolonial Asia not by pouring oil on the fires of religious conflict and violence and engaging in competitive apologetics and aggressive proselytism against the practitioners of other religions. Instead, the Asian church seeks to break the impasse by going beyond the superficiality of quantitative church growth in favor of a qualitative *prophetic* approach that is able to transform and heal the violence and brokenness in a continent that is being torn apart by wars and conflicts in the name of exclusivist fanaticism and exceptionalism.

A Postcolonial Asian Ecclesiology

In his analysis of the FABC's ecclesiology, Peter C. Phan characterizes it as a "sort of Copernican revolution in ecclesiology" that "sees the goal and purpose of the mission of the church to be not the geographical and institutional expansion of the church (the *plantatio ecclesiae*)" but "a transparent sign of and effective instrument for the saving presence of the reign of God, the reign of justice, peace, and love, of which the church is a seed" (2003a, 14). Phan also notes that the FABC has consciously avoided "churchy themes such as papal primacy and infallibility, apostolic succession, magisterium, Episcopal power, the hierarchical structure, canon law, the Roman Curia, women's ordination, and the like" in favor of a regnocentric way of being church that seeks to implement, pastorally and spiritually, the ways "that are appropriate to the socio-political, economic, cultural, and religious contexts of Asia" (2018, 15). Phan's incisive observation summarizes succinctly the FABC's vision of a new way of being church in Asia by being a participatory, dialogical, and prophetic church that seeks to immerse itself in the postcolonial Asian milieu in solidarity and empathy with the subaltern Asian peoples and the fullness of their daily lived experiences.

In doing so, the FABC unequivocally privileges solidarity, companionship, and collaborative partnership with the Asian peoples and their diverse cultures, many religions, and experiences of immense poverty. As far as the FABC is concerned, it is "the local churches and communities which can discern and work (in dialogue with each other and with other persons of goodwill) the way the Gospel is best proclaimed, the Church set up, the values of God's Kingdom realized in their own place and time. In fact, it is by responding to and serving the needs of the peoples of Asia that the different Christian communities become truly local Churches" (FABC V, 3.3.1, in Rosales and Arévalo 1992, 281).

Unsurprisingly, the FABC expresses its unambiguous preference for a qualitative ecclesiology that seeks to transform and heal the brokenness in postcolonial Asian realities rather than a quantitative ecclesiology that emphasizes growth in terms of numerical and territorial expansion of the institutional church. Here it is noteworthy that the FABC perceives the Asian church as remaining a "little flock" amid the cultural diversity and religious plurality of postcolonial Asia for the foreseeable future. Within this understanding, the FABC sees Asian Christians as religious minorities who are amid the majorities of other religious traditions and are able to witness to the redemptive power of the Christian gospel by the example and testimony of their daily living in companionship, empathy, and solidarity with their neighbors across religious boundaries, working, struggling, and suffering as fellow humans on a common quest for the meaning of life. Seen in this light, inculturation, interreligious dialogue, and human liberation are not mere preevangelistic activities but rather integral dimensions of the FABC's mission theology of "active integral evangelization." What is more, the FABC is convinced that "if Asian churches do not discover their own identity, they will have no future" (*Asian Colloquium on Ministries in the Church*, 14[ii], in Rosales and Arévalo 1992, 70). For the FABC, the way forward is not a defensive and inward-looking church but a church that seeks to collaborate with others to address the challenges of Asia in the twenty-first century.

5

Coming of Age at the Asian Synod

In 1995, the Synod of Bishops' secretary-general, Cardinal Jan P. Schotte, announced the Special Assembly of the Synod of Bishops for Asia. This announcement was made in response to Pope John Paul II's call in his apostolic letter *Tertio millennio adveniente* (1994) for, among other things, special synods from different parts of the world to prepare for the coming of the third Christian millennium. The Asian Synod brought together for the very first time three broad and disparate communities of churches with their historically unique and ritually distinctive ecclesial traditions, sharing only the adjective *Asian*. In addition to the Federation of Asian Bishops' Conferences (FABC), the other two groups are the ancient apostolic *sui iuris* churches of West Asia (the birthplace and ancient cradle of Christianity), which are united under the aegis of the Council of Catholic Patriarchs of the East (Le Conseil des Patriarches Catholiques d'Orient, or CPCO) and the two Eastern Catholic churches in India—that is, the Syro-Malabar Catholic Church and Syro-Malankara Catholic Church.[1]

Established in 1991 and meeting once a year in regular session, the CPCO comprises the communion and patriarchal collegiality of the seven Eastern Catholic patriarchs of West Asia. In order of precedent, dignity, and honor, these seven patriarchs are (1) the patriarch of Antioch and all the East for the Maronite Catholic Church, (2) the Coptic Catholic patriarch of Alexandria, (3) the patriarch of Antioch and all the East, Alexandria, and Jerusalem for the Melkite Greek Catholic Church, (4) the patriarch of Antioch and all the East for the Syrian Catholic Church, (5) the patriarch of Babylon for the Chaldean Catholic Church, (6) the patriarch (catholicos) of Cilicia for the Armenian Catholic Church, and (7) the Latin patriarch of Jerusalem.[2] Strictly speaking, the CPCO is not a council or federation of bishops' conferences, unlike the FABC or the Latin American Episcopal Conference (Consejo Episcopal Latinoamericano, or CELAM). Rather, it is both a communion of all of the seven Catholic patriarchs in the East as well as a sign and an instrument of patriarchal collegiality.

The Indian subcontinent is home to three Catholic churches *sui iuris*: Latin Catholic, as represented by the Conference of Catholic Bishops of India (CCBI), together with the Syro-Malabar Church and the Syro-Malankara Church, both of which are heirs to the ancient apostolic Saint Thomas Christians of Malabar, India.[3] What is unique in the Indian context is that all three churches *sui iuris*—Syro-Malabar, Syro-Malankara, and Latin Catholic (CCBI)—are full members of the Catholic Bishops' Conference of India (CBCI)[4] while retaining their distinct hierarchical and ecclesial identities. By virtue of their membership in the CBCI, both the Syro-Malabar Church and the Syro-Malankara Church are also members of as well as participate in the activities of the FABC. For example, the late Moran Mor Cyril Baselios, who served as the major archbishop and catholicos of the Syro-Malankara Church, was also a member of the FABC Standing Committee.

More importantly, the Asian Synod also enabled bishops across the east-west ecclesial divide and from across the different regions of Asia to collaborate and work together for the first time in a moment of pan-Asian solidarity and collegiality (Prior 1998, 657). Never before have Asian bishops from the ancient churches of West Asia that constitute the CPCO as well as the nascent churches of the Central Asian republics and the local churches of postcolonial East, South, and Southeast Asia that make up the FABC met and collaborated in a visible sign of ecclesial unity. While they may come from different social, cultural, and ecclesial backgrounds, the bishops of the CPCO and FABC all share one thing in common—they represent churches that are minorities in their own milieus, with the exception of the Philippines and Timor-Leste. Hence the Asian Synod presented a historic opportunity for the FABC and CPCO to mutually support each other, as well as share and learn from each other's experiences about common concerns, issues, and strategies for being church and witnessing the gospel message in Asia.

Composition of Synodal Delegates and Commissions

A total of 252 delegates were listed as participants in the Asian Synod, of which 188 had full voting rights and the remaining 64 were nonvoting participants. Those with full voting rights consisted of 67 ex officio delegates, 98 *ex electione* delegates, and 23 *ex nominatione pontificia* special delegates. The nonvoting delegates consisted of 18 synodal experts (*auditores secretarii specialis*), 40 synodal auditors (*auditores*), and 6 ecumenical delegates. In addition to these 252 delegates, the Eastern Catholic patriarchs of the CPCO, Asian cardinals, presidents of the FABC member conferences, heads of nonpatriarchal Eastern Catholic churches *sui iuris*, FABC secretary-general, heads of ecclesiastical territories without an episcopal conference (i.e., Macau, Timor-Leste, Kazakhstan, Kyrgyzstan, Nepal, Tajikistan, Turkmenistan, Uzbekistan, and Mongolia), general secretary of the Synod of Bishops (Cardinal Jan Schotte), and heads of the various departments of the Roman Curia also participated as ex officio members (Bali 1998, 298; Prior 1998, 654; Union of Catholic Asian News [UCAN] 1998d).

All churches *sui iuris* and episcopal conferences were permitted to nominate a proportional number of *ex electione* delegates to the Asian Synod in the following manner: churches *sui iuris* and episcopal conferences with fewer than one hundred bishops chose one delegate for every seven bishops, and those with fewer than one hundred bishops chose one delegate for every ten bishops (Claver 1998, 242). Not surprisingly, the two largest contingents were from India (twenty-seven delegates from all three churches *sui iuris*: Latin, Syro-Malabar, and Syro-Malankara) and the Philippines (seventeen delegates, of which thirteen were elected and four were conference presidents; Claver 1998, 242). An additional ten *ex electione* delegates were elected by the Union of Superior Generals of male religious orders.

The twenty-three *ex nominatione pontificia* special delegates who were selected by Pope John II included sixteen additional bishops (seven from Asia, five from the Americas, three from Europe, and one from Africa), one FABC representative, three religious order priests from Asia (one each from the Franciscans, Jesuits, and Benedictines), and three curial presidents. These special members were Salesian Archbishop Thomas Menamparampil (Guwahati, India), Bishop Anthony Theodore Lobo (Islamabad-Rawalpindi, Pakistan), Bishop Joseph Vianney Fernando (Kandy, Sri Lanka), Bishop Andrew Tsien Tchew-choenn (Hualien, Taiwan), Salesian Coadjutor Bishop Joseph Zen Ze-kiun (Hong Kong), Auxiliary Bishop John Tong Hon (Hong Kong), Msgr. Cornelius Sim (apostolic prefect, Brunei-Darussalam), Fr. Edward Malone (FABC assistant secretary-general),

Fr. Oscar Ante (provincial minister Order of the Friars Minor, Philippines), Benedictine Abbot John Kurichianil (India), and Fr. Paul Tan Chee Ing (Jesuit assistant general for East Asia). The sole representative from Africa was Archbishop Wilfrid Fox Napier (Durban, South Africa). Members from the Americas were Archbishop Adam Exner (Vancouver, British Columbia, Canada), Bishop Benedict Singh (Georgetown, Guyana), Bishop Emilio Pignoli (Campo Limpo, Brazil), Bishop John Cummins (Oakland, California), and Bishop Francis Xavier DiLorenzo (Honolulu, Hawai'i). Members from Europe were Bishop Gilbert Aubry (Saint-Denis-de-La Réunion), Bishop Martinus Petrus Maria Muskens (Breda, Netherlands), and Auxiliary Bishop Reinhard Marx (Paderborn, Germany). Members from the Vatican were Archbishop Francis Xavier Nguyen Van Thuan (vice president, Pontifical Council for Justice and Peace), Archbishop Francesco Marchisano (president, Pontifical Commission for the Cultural Heritage of the Church), and Holy Cross Archbishop Charles Schleck (president, Pontifical Missionary Works). Statistically, of the ten special members from Asia, four were from the Indian subcontinent, three were from Northeast Asia, and three were from Southeast Asia.

The pope also appointed three Synod president delegates to moderate the sessions—Cardinal Stephen Kim Sou-hwan (Seoul, Korea), Cardinal Jozef Tomko (prefect of the Congregation for the Evangelization of Peoples), and Cardinal Julius Riyadi Darmaatmadja (Jakarta, Indonesia), assisted by Cardinal Paul Shan Kuo-hsi (Kaohsiung, Taiwan) as the relator general and Archbishop Thomas Menamparampil as the synod special secretary (UCAN 1998e). Finally, Archbishop Oscar V. Cruz (Lingayen-Dagupan, Philippines; the FABC general secretary) and Bishop Anthony Theodore Lobo were appointed the president and vice president of the Commission for the Message, while Bishop Joseph Vianney Fernando and Melkite Greek Archbishop Cyrille Salim Bustros (Baalbek, Lebanon) were appointed the president and vice president of the Commission for Information, respectively.

Three other commissions were also set up to take care of particular needs of the Asian Synod. First, the Commission for Controversies was formed to study and propose solutions for theological disputes. Its three presidents were Cardinal Gilberto Agustoni (prefect, Supreme Tribunal of the Apostolic Signatura), Maronite Archbishop Paul Youssef Matar (Beirut, Lebanon), and Bishop Martinus Dogma Situmorang (Padang, Indonesia). The Commission for Information took charge of all major press conferences and daily press briefings in collaboration with the Holy See Press Office. Led by Bishop Vianney Fernando and Melkite Greek Archbishop Cyrille Salim Bustros, its members were Archbishop Orlando Quevedo (Nueva Segovia, Philippines), Archbishop Alan Basil de Lastic (Delhi, India), Archbishop Thomas Menamparampil, Bishop Michael Bunluen Mansap (Ubon Ratchathani, Thailand), Bishop John Chang Yik (Chunchon, South Korea), Auxiliary Bishop Theotonius Gomes (Dhaka, Bangladesh), Auxiliary Bishop John Tong Hon, and Immaculate Heart of Mary Fr. Wenceslao Padilla (superior, *sui iuris* Mission of Urga in Mongolia). Fr. John Mansford Prior, the Divine Word missioner, was in charge of conducting the daily English-language press briefings. A Commission for the Message was set up to prepare the final message, which was released on the last day of the synodal proceedings, and comprised the following: Archbishop Oscar V. Cruz as president and Bishop Anthony Theodore Lobo as vice president, together with Archbishop Peter Chung Hoan Ting (Kuching, Malaysia), Archbishop Telesphore Toppo (Ranchi, India), Archbishop Leo Jun Ikenaga (Osaka, Japan), Bishop Yves Ramousse (apostolic vicar of Phnom Penh, Cambodia), Chaldean Bishop Antoine Audo (Alep, Syria), Bishop Martinus Petrus Maria Muskens, Coadjutor Bishop Joseph Zen Ze-kiun, Fr. Alexander Kahn (superior, *sui iuris* Mission of Kyrgyzstan), and Fr. Raymond Rossignol (superior general, Paris Foreign Missions Society) as members.

From the onset, it was clear that this was going to be strictly a *synod of bishops*. Lay representation was a minuscule 8 percent of the delegates, to say the least. Of the forty observers, only twenty were lay (twelve laymen and eight laywomen). Similarly, women formed an even smaller contingent. Out of a total of seventeen women (nine religious and eight lay) who participated in the synod, sixteen were synodal observers, and one lone woman religious was among the seventeen synodal experts (UCAN 1998d). It was regrettable that a lone observer, twenty-two-year-old Nicholas Somchai Tharaphan, who was the president of the Catholic Student Association of Bangkok and the youngest participant at the Asian Synod, represented the entire youth population of the Asian churches. While lay delegates could attend and address the assembly, as well as participate in small group discussions, nevertheless as mere auditors (*auditores*), they could not vote on the synodal decisions or documents.

Finally, an important fifteen-member Post-Synodal Council to assist Pope John Paul II in his writing of the postsynodal apostolic exhortation was announced by Cardinal Schotte on May 8, 1998. Headed by Cardinal Jozef Tomko, the council comprised eleven prelates from the FABC member conferences and three from Central and West Asia. Representing the FABC member conferences were Cardinal Julius Riyadi Darmaatmadja, Cardinal Paul Shan Kuohsi, Archbishop Oscar V. Cruz, Syro-Malabar Archbishop Joseph Powathil (Changanacherry, India), Archbishop Alan Basil de Lastic, Archbishop Matthias U Shwe (Taunggyi, Myanmar), Bishop Stephen Fumio Hamao (Yokohama, Japan), Bishop Paul Nguyen Van Hoa (Nha Trang, Vietnam), Bishop George Yod Phimphisan (Udon Thani, Thailand), Bishop Joseph Vianney Fernando, and Coadjutor Bishop Joseph Zen Ze-kiun, while the three prelates from Central and West Asia were the Latin Patriarch Michel Sabbah (Jerusalem), Chaldean Bishop Antoine Audo, and Bishop Jan Pawel Lenga (apostolic administrator of Kazakhstan). Of the fifteen, three were appointed by the pope—Cardinal Tomko, Bishop Lenga, and Bishop Zen. In regional terms, Southeast Asia had the biggest representation with five members (Indonesia, Myanmar, Philippines, Thailand, and Vietnam), followed by three each from East Asia (China, Japan, and Taiwan) and South Asia (two from India, one from Sri Lanka). West Asia had two representatives (Jerusalem and Syria), while Central Asia had one (Kazakhstan). Cardinal Tomko was the Vatican's sole representative. Three of the council members were Jesuits (Cardinal Darmaatmadja, Cardinal Shan, and Bishop Audo), one was a Redemptorist (Bishop Phimphisan), one a Salesian (Bishop Zen), and one a Marian missioner (Bishop Lenga).

Initial Responses to the Synod Theme

The theme of the Asian Synod—"Jesus Christ the Saviour and His Mission of Love and Service in Asia: '. . . That They May Have Life, and Have It Abundantly'"—reflects Pope John Paul II's grave concern regarding the lack of church growth in Asia other than in the Philippines and Timor-Leste. The synod's introductory document, or *Lineamenta*, provides an overview of the synod's theme and issues, together with fourteen questions on the challenges of religious pluralism for doing Christian mission and evangelization in contemporary Asia for the Asian Catholic bishops' consideration and response (General Secretariat of the Synod of Bishops 1997; Phan 2002, 13–16). The *Lineamenta* emphasizes that God's salvific design is manifested in Jesus Christ, and therefore, "the church in Asia has and wants to proclaim Jesus Christ to her brothers and sisters on the continent so that they may be enriched by the inexhaustible riches of Jesus Christ" (art. 21, in General Secretariat of the Synod of Bishops 1997, 510). It specifically criticizes the FABC's focus on dialogue in response to religious pluralism, as we have seen in chapter 4, instead of focusing on the proclamation of the gospel (art. 30, in General Secretariat of the Synod of Bishops 1997, 514), insisting, "The primacy of the proclamation of Jesus

Christ in all evangelizing activities has been repeatedly stressed by the council and the magisterium of the church because it is of the essence of the faith and the very continuation of the saving event of Jesus Christ" (art. 31, General Secretariat of the Synod of Bishops in 1997, 514). In their responses to the *Lineamenta*, many Asian Catholic bishops take issue with its uncompromising emphasis on the proclamation of the gospel as the principal task of doing Christian mission and evangelization in Asia, as well as challenge its negativity toward dialogue with Asian religions and acceptance of religious pluralism in postcolonial Asia.

South Asia: India and Sri Lanka

While recognizing that "in union with the Father and the Spirit, Christ is indeed the source and cause of salvation for all peoples," the CBCI is adamant that "this fact does not exclude the possibility of God mysteriously employing other cooperating channels" (art. 5.1, in CBCI 1998, 121; Phan 2002, 21). The CBCI also contends that the *Lineamenta*'s emphasis on Jesus Christ as the one and only savior should be understood "in a way that takes seriously into account the multicultural and multireligious situations" of the Indian context (art. 5.1, in CBCI 1998, 121; Phan 2002, 22). In addition, the CBCI strenuously argues against an exclusivist understanding of salvation and makes the case for the soteriological dimensions of other Asian religions, explaining,

> In the light of the universal salvific will and design of God, so emphatically affirmed in the New Testament witness, the Indian Christological approach seeks to avoid negative and exclusivistic expression. Christ is a Sacrament, a definitive Symbol, of God's salvation for the entire humanity. This is what the salvific uniqueness and universality of Christ means in the Indian context. That,

however, does not mean there cannot be other symbols, valid in their own ways, which the Christian sees as related to the definitive Symbol, Jesus Christ. *The implication of all this is that for hundreds of millions of our fellow human beings, salvation is seen as being channeled to them not in spite of but through and in their various sociocultural and religious traditions. We cannot, then, deny, a priori, a salvific role for these non-Christian religions.* (art. 5.1, in CBCI 1998, 121; Phan 2002, 22; emphasis added)

Here the CBCI's response reiterates the point that the Indian Theological Association makes in its position paper *The Significance of Jesus Christ in the Context of Religious Pluralism in India* (April 1998):

In the context of our positive experience of other believers in their search for and realization of wholeness and freedom, we acknowledge the gracious and loving act of God who has reached out to them in various ways. . . . Celebrating this gracious and living mystery of God, we are not only aware of the Spirit of God "who blows where She wills," but also of the Word of God who speaks to peoples through various manifestations in different ways (Heb 1:1), and whom we profess as the one who became incarnate in Jesus. We gratefully acknowledge that it is our experience of the incarnate Jesus that leads us to the discovery of the cosmic dimensions of the presence and action of the Word. . . . *For the Christian believer, Jesus Christ is the perfect symbol of God who brings fulfilment to all persons in their world through his words and works, signs and wonders. He is unique to the Christian in that he is the definitive, though non-exhaustive symbol of God-experience in the world.* But Jesus' uniqueness *does*

not necessarily displace symbols in other religions. . . .
The vision of all the saving movements in the world as
manifestations of the one divine mystery, of the one
Word and the one Spirit of God, urges us to be open to the
religious experience of others and to dialogue with
them. . . . We hear the call of Jesus to contribute through
the process of dialogue and convergence to a growing
reconciliation and peace with justice. (5.14–5.20, quoted in
Amaladoss 2000, 235–36; emphasis added)

The Sri Lankan Catholic bishops agree with their Indian counterparts on the need to situate Jesus and his gospel within the religious pluralism of Sri Lanka, explaining that Sri Lankan Catholics
"live in a multireligious setting in which Jesus Christ is viewed in
many different forms: Muslims accept Jesus as a great prophet as
he is mentioned in the Koran. Hindus treat him as an avatar, an
incarnation of God. Buddhists see him as a social reformer and a
great teacher, and for many others he is a great liberator. Generally
speaking, there seems to be an awesome respect for Jesus Christ"
(Phan 2002, 42–43).

Japan

The Japanese Catholic bishops detect a tone of "defensiveness"
toward religious pluralism in the *Lineamenta*. With the benefit
of the lived experiences of being a religious minority in Japan, making
up only about 0.5 percent of the Japanese population, the Japanese
Catholic bishops contend that religious pluralism could be a learning experience for the church. Specifically, while they accept that
"Jesus Christ is the Way, the Truth and the Life," they clarify that in
the Japanese context, "before stressing that Jesus Christ is the
Truth, we must search much more deeply into how he is the Way
and the Life. If we stress too much that 'Jesus Christ is the One and

Only Savior,' we can have no dialogue, common living, or solidarity with other religions. The Church, learning from the *kenosis* of Jesus Christ, should be humble and *open its heart to other religions to deepen its understanding of the Mystery of Christ*" (1998, 89; Phan 2002, 30; emphasis added).

Moreover, the Japanese Catholic bishops argue that the *Lineamenta*'s condemnation of dialogue as a response to religious pluralism and uncompromising insistence on mission as the "proclamation of Christ" is counterproductive in the plurireligious Japanese context, explaining the need for collaboration and "creative harmony" in any dialogue between the Christian gospel and other religions in Japan. They note that the *Lineamenta* emphasizes "(as in traditional scholastic theology) . . . 'distinctions' and 'differences'" and point out that in the Japanese context, it "is characteristic to search for creative harmony rather than distinctions" (Japanese Catholic bishops 1998, 90; Phan 2002, 31). On the issue of lack of church growth, the Japanese Catholic bishops push back against a quantitative focus on church growth using metrics such as the "number of baptisms" and "a 'success orientation' of 'trying for better results,'" making the argument instead for the necessity of "a vision of evangelization that gives joy and a sense of purpose to a Christian living as one of a minority in the midst of many traditional religions" in contemporary Japan (1998, 90; Phan 2002, 31). They remind the Vatican of the "limits felt to the 'Western-type' of missionary activity used up to now," which have not produced the desired church growth despite centuries of missionary activity, and advocate instead for the articulation of an Asian spirituality and inculturation of the Christian gospel in a spirit of dialogue and harmony with other religions in contemporary Japan (Japanese Catholic bishops 1998, 91–92).

Southeast Asia: Indonesia and Vietnam

The Indonesian Catholic bishops observe that "Jesus does not exclusively belong to Christians, because He is acknowledged and respected by people of other faiths also" (art. 5.3.4, in Indonesian Catholic bishops 1998, 67). In their own words, "In pluri-religious societies it is often difficult to directly and explicitly proclaim the central role of Jesus Christ in the economy of salvation. This proclamation must be adapted to concrete life conditions and to the disposition of the hearers. Evangelization ought to start from a 'common ground,' i.e., belief in the Supreme being as taught by well-respected spiritual leaders and as explicitly stated among the 'Five Principles' (Pancasila)" (art. 5.1.5, in Indonesian Catholic bishops 1998, 64–65).

In a similar vein, the Vietnamese Catholic bishops speak positively of religious pluralism in the Asian continent and the soteriological efficacy of other religions, insisting that the task of evangelization in Vietnam does not begin on a clean slate but rather builds on the presence of existing religions whose vitality could help illumine the gospel:

The Church in Vietnam believes it must rethink its ways of evangelizing in Asia. The first reason is that this continent is not virgin or fallow soil on which any kind of seed can be sown. Rather, it is a land of very ancient religions and civilizations when compared to Europe. It is a spiritual font of rich and solid ideas about the universe, humanity, and religion. Its peoples are not without knowledge of God. Quite the opposite, they have a certain experience of his presence and invoke him under different names such as "Sky," "Heaven," "Brahman," etc. *Consequently, to "evangelize" in this particular case does not mean to present a God, a Christ, as totally unknown, but, in a*

certain way—to borrow a Buddhist expression—it is to
"make the Light shine more brightly," present but hidden;
it is to help people "see the Truth illuminated," which
Vatican II recognizes as partially present in other religions,
especially those of Asia. (Phan 2002, 48; emphasis added)

Synod Opening and Proceedings

The Asian Synod met in Rome from April 19 to May 14, 1998, opening with a solemn Eucharist concelebrated by the pope with six patriarchs, thirty-four cardinals, forty-nine archbishops, seventy-eight bishops, and ninety-two priests in Saint Peter's Basilica. Although Latin and Italian were the two principal languages of this Eucharist, an effort was nevertheless made to represent the rich cultural and linguistic diversity of the Asian churches throughout the liturgy, marking a momentous milestone in the celebration of an inculturated Asian liturgy of the Eucharist for the first time at Saint Peter's Basilica.

To illustrate, the Gloria was sung in Filipino using Jesuit Fr. Eduardo Hontiveros's setting of "Papuri sa Diyos" ("Praise be to God"), the gospel was proclaimed in Malayalam according to the Syro-Malabar liturgical ritual, and the General Intercessions were read in Arabic, Chinese, Filipino, Korean, Tamil, and Vietnamese. The highlight of the preparation of the gifts was a Batak Tor-Tor dance of joy and thanksgiving accompanying the eucharistic gifts that was performed by a dance troupe of Indonesian men and women carrying flowers, incense, and candles to the Indonesian hymn "Bawalah Persembahan" ("Let us bring forth our gifts"). This dramatic moment was labeled an unprecedented event by Vatican observers (Fox 1998b). At the Great Amen of the eucharistic prayer, an Indian dance troupe performed the *arti* love dance for the arrival of a spouse. In addition, the cover of the worship program was decorated with Christian artwork in Chinese style from an early twentieth-century collection of the now defunct Catholic University of Peking. In his homily, Pope John Paul II alluded to Saint John's task of writing the book of Revelation and sending it to the seven churches of Asia, saying that the synod's work "will be compiled in a book, which will be the post-Synodal document for all the Churches in Asia" and in which "will be written what the Spirit suggests." The pope also emphasized the need for a "fresh missionary outreach" to "bear witness to what the Spirit says" to the Asian peoples and cultures (Hebblethwaite 1998a).

Following the opening Eucharist, the synod's first week began on April 20, 1998, with the presentation of the *Relatio ante discepⁿ tationem* by Cardinal Paul Shan, the synod's relator general. Cardinal Shan acknowledged the difficulty of many Asians to accept Christ as a unique savior and suggested that an Asian Christology should center "on the 'self-emptying' of Jesus in his Incarnation, Passion and death and his being 'filled up' in the mystery of the Resurrection." He explained that a "suffering servant of the Lord, who shares the pain, poverty, rejection and exploitation of the Asian peoples" and is "able to give them a sense of human dignity will be appealing to the heart of Asia" (Hebblethwaite 1998a). Cardinal Shan also pointed out that both the "degrading poverty, inequality and social injustice" in the Asian milieu as well as the Asian people's "great hunger for spiritual and religious values, freedom, human dignity and advancement" call for "a new evangelization" such that the Asian church is "not only a Church for the poor, but also a Church with the poor" (1998a). He reminded everyone present that the "Church in Asia needs to keep in mind that ultimately it is not doctrinal arguments which will make the person of Jesus Christ appealing and acceptable to Asian peoples; the witness given by Christians to Jesus Christ will be convincing" (1998a).

The synod's daily plenary sessions consisted of fourteen general congregations, one each in the morning and afternoon for the next seven days. Notwithstanding the fact that twenty-seven Asian languages were represented at the synod, the two official languages of the synod were English and French, two non-Asian languages. Cardinal Schotte explained in a presynodal news conference that it was not feasible to introduce Asian languages because there were too many of them (Fox 1998b). All the synod fathers and other synodal participants were divided into eleven small groups (*circuli minores*), comprising eight English groups, two French groups, and one Italian group (Tagle 1998, 368). These small groups met from the second week onward for more extensive deliberations on key ideas, concepts, and issues. The moderators of the two French small groups were the Maronite Catholic archbishop Joseph Mohsen Bechara (Antelias, Lebanon) and the Armenian archbishop Boutros Marayati (Alep, Syria), while Archbishop Joseph Ti-kang (Taipei, Taiwan) moderated the sole Italian group. The eight English small groups were led by Bishop Valerian D'Souza (Poona, India), Bishop Patrick D'Souza (Varanasi, India), Archbishop Henry D'Souza (Calcutta, India), Archbishop Alan Basil de Lastic, Archbishop Alberto Piamonte (Jaro, Philippines), Bishop Oswald Gomis (Anuradhapura, Sri Lanka), Bishop George Yod Phimphisan, and Cardinal Edward Cassidy (president, Pontifical Council for Promoting Christian Unity).

A total of 191 oral "rapid-fire" interventions were presented by the synod fathers, experts, and observers during the first week and a half of the synodal proceedings. This nonstop marathon left many participants feeling exhausted and overstuffed (Prior 1998, 656–57; Hebblethwaite 1998c, 599; Fox 1998a, 13). Unlike previous synods where delegates could speak as often as they wanted, for the first time, in the name of synodal efficiency, all the delegates at the Asian Synod were only permitted to speak once during the entire synod (Claver 1998, 242–43). These interventions were strictly timed eight-minute presentations for the synod fathers and five minutes for all other participants. Participants who went beyond the allotted time found their microphones cut off abruptly (Fox 1998a, 13). Not only did these nonstop interventions leave no room for any discussion or pause for reflection; the interventions were scheduled on a "first-come-first-served" basis without any particular thematic order.

Of the 191 interventions, only three bishops spoke directly on the synod's official theme, and two of these three bishops were curial bishops (Fox 1998c). The Vatican-appointed director of the English section of the Asian Synod Press Office, John Mansford Prior, analyzed all 191 interventions of the Asian Catholic bishops and categorized them as follows: "Seventy-six percent of the interventions dealt with four Asian topics. At the top of the list comes the mission of the Asian churches to *dialogue with other faith traditions* (43 interventions, or 22.5% of the total). Second in frequency comes *dialogue with living cultures* by which the Church becomes truly Asian (41 interventions, or 21.4% of the total). At number three comes the *dialogue of the churches with the poor* (33 interventions, or 17.2%). At fourth place, the interventions characterized the Asian Churches as *churches of the laity* (29 interventions, or 15.2%)" (Prior 1998, 658; emphasis added).

Responding to Religious Pluralism

Many Asian Catholic bishops brought to the forefront the issue of religious pluralism in their synod interventions, speaking eloquently in support of the FABC's preferred approach of dialogue with other religions in response to the challenges of religious pluralism. For example, Bishop Paul Nguyen Van Hoa explained that since the majority of Asians belong to ancient religious and cultural traditions, it was necessary to reflect on interreligious dialogue as evangelization (Phan 2002, 124; UCAN 1998a). For Cardinal Peter Seiichi Shirayanagi (Tokyo), religion will touch the lives of people deeply and answer their deepest longings when the dialogue of theological discourse, religious experience, and life takes place (UCAN 1998a). According to Fr. Alex Ukken, prior general of the Carmelites of the Immaculate Virgin Mary, "The Church will become a powerful moral force in Asia even as a minority religion, if it enters into interreligious dialogue, evangelizes cultures, and transforms unjust and inhuman social and political structures" (UCAN 1998f). Bishop Bunluen Mansap highlighted the benefits of Christian-Buddhist interreligious dialogue in Thailand, saying that he felt "inspired by their simplicity of life, their openness, their humane relationships, their unassuming ways," acknowledging that he recognized these values as "values of the Kingdom or the Gospel," and wondering whether this could be the good news that the Buddhists could offer to Asian Catholics (Prior 1998, 659; Phan 2002, 121).

The issue of interreligious dialogue took on added urgency in the context of Christian-Muslim dialogue. As expected, the synod fathers from the Muslim majority countries in Asia were very concerned with the impact of Islam on minority Christian communities. Chaldean Archbishop Yousif Thomas Mirkis (Beirut, Lebanon) emphasized the urgency of genuine interreligious dialogue between Muslims and Christians to promote peaceful coexistence between these two religious communities and the self-preservation of the Christian minority (UCAN 1998f). Bishop Joseph Coutts (Hyderabad, Pakistan) brought the synod's attention to the challenges arising from the increasing militancy and intolerance of many Muslims toward minority Christian communities in Islamic countries (UCAN 1998f). Bishop Leo Laba Ladjar (Jayapura, Indonesia) suggested that the Christian minority in Indonesia should not only accept their minority status but also move beyond confrontation to find ways of coexisting peacefully and harmoniously with the Muslim majority, saying, "We need to accept ourselves as a minority. We cannot walk alone or do big things alone while confronting the majority. Competition does not help to create peace and harmony. Whatever we do to promote human dignity we must do as an honest transparent service to humankind and not to gain strength and power for our own religious group" (Prior 1998, 659).

In relation to the Christian gospel's dialogue with Asian cultures, Bishop Berard Oshikawa (Naha, Japan) put forward his arguments for a harmonious "graduality" in the Holy See's role of safeguarding orthodoxy in theology and liturgical practice:

> It seems to me that the norm for Christian life, for Church discipline, for liturgical expression and theological orthodoxy continues to be that of the Western Church. The language of our theology, the rhythm and structure of our liturgies, the programmes of our catechesis fail to touch the hearts of those who come searching. . . . Graduality means that the Holy See redefine its role and with prudence, flexibility, trust and courage mediate a new dialogue of all the churches in the common pilgrimage to the fullness of Christ, moving away from a single and uniform abstract norm that stifles genuine spirituality; working for a new harmony where the gifts of the Spirit to the churches become the new treasure of the whole church. (Prior 1998, 660)

Bishop Francis Xavier Sudartanta Hadisumarta (Manokwari-Sorong, Indonesia) argued the need for a "radical decentralisation of the Latin Rite" (Prior 1998, 660). Bishop Benedict John Osta (Patna, India) suggested that "instead of spending energies in translating the official texts, we need to promote creativity in the cultural context of Asia" (UCAN 1998a). The superior general of the Missionaries of the Holy Family, Fr. Wilhelmus van der Weiden, challenged the Roman dicasteries on the issue of liturgical inculturation: "Are the Roman *dicasteries* so afraid for aberrations from that which is considered as the only true doctrine and the only true formulation of the liturgy? Must we not say that often the bishops' conferences with 20, 30 or more bishops and a number of theologians and specialists can better estimate what in liturgical matters is best for their flock than Roman authorities who often don't know the language and the culture of that country?" (Fox 1998c).

Without any doubt, the highlight of the synodal interventions was that of Carmelite Bishop Hadisumarta. Speaking on behalf of the Indonesian Catholic Bishops' Conference, he caused a great stir when he argued strenuously that "what we need is trust: trust in God and trust in each other. Bishops are not branch secretaries waiting for instructions from headquarters. We are a communion of local churches" (Fox 1998a, 14). Bishop Hadisumarta also voiced aloud the view shared by many of his confreres that the Roman curia should become "a clearinghouse for information, support and encouragement rather than a universal decision-maker" (Fox 1998a, 14). He concluded his intervention with a skillfully delivered coup de grâce: "Do we have the imagination to envisage the birth of new patriarchates . . . and a radical decentralization of the Latin Rite—devolving into a host of local rites in Asia . . . say the patriarchate of South Asia, of Southeast Asia and of East Asia?" (UCAN 1998g; Fox 1998a, 14). Apparently, this statement elicited a very forceful nonverbal reaction from Cardinal Schotte: "If glares could kill, he would have died instantly," someone said of the look on Cardinal Schotte's face (Hebblethwaite 1998c, 600).

The question of ecclesial autonomy also featured strongly in the interventions of the Eastern Catholic bishops belonging to the patriarchal churches of the CPCO. The Melkite Greek archbishop Cyrille Salim Bustros called for a retrieval of the ancient tradition of autocephaly in Eastern Catholic churches. Bishop Bustros pointed out that by ancient custom, the appointment of bishops was the prerogative and privilege of the patriarchs. According to him, while the pope, by virtue of being the "Patriarch of the West," has the prerogative to appoint bishops in Latin Catholic churches, this right does not ipso facto extend to the Eastern Catholic churches. On this basis, he put forward three requests to the pope: "election of bishops without recourse to Rome, creating of dioceses outside the Orient without recourse to Rome, and the freedom to have married clergy in Oriental dioceses established in the West" (Hebblethwaite 1998c, 600; Fox 1998a, 13–14).

Relating religious pluralism to the task of doing Christian mission in Asia, many synod fathers argued that there must be authentic witnessing that would embed the gospel in people's life experiences as the starting point rather than the abstract and intellectual proclamation of doctrines and norms of orthodoxy. Bishop Leo Laba Ladjar argued that such an aggressive "superior attitude" has "long humiliated the Muslim majority" (UCAN 1998g). Archbishop Ignatius Suharyo Hardjoatmodjo (Semarang, Indonesia) informed the synod that in doing Christian mission in Asia, "we do not start with the Church, which is often mistakenly identified with the great display of institutions, but with what the Spirit is doing in people, religions and cultures" of Asia (UCAN 1998g).

Arguing along similar lines, the Syro-Malabar Bishop Gratian Mundadan (Bijnor, India) explained that "in the religious ethos of Asia mere doctrinal, legal and institutional power does not have any appeal. Further, the image projected by the Church of power, riches, institutional, influential, is looked upon as a threat" (Prior 1998, 663; Phan 2002, 111). According to Archbishop Johannes Liku Ada (Ujung Pandang, Indonesia), mission and evangelization in the Asian context meant the ability to unearth what is true, good, and beautiful in the Asian religions, "even the Spirit at work in them" (UCAN 1998g). Such sentiments were also voiced by Bishop Augustine Jun-ichi Nomura (Nagoya, Japan): "In Japan, like the rest of Asia, the eyes have a more central role than the ears in the process of insight and conversion. . . . [The Asian peoples] are convinced more by witnessing than by teaching, and . . . they appreciate the contemplative dimension, detachment, humility, simplicity and silence" (UCAN 1998g).

Following the conclusion of the synod's interventions on April 28th, Cardinal Shan presented the forty-three-page *Relatio post disceptationem*, which summarized all the interventions and identified issues for discussion in the small groups. A controversy erupted over this *relatio*, which supposedly summarized all the interventions but was apparently completed on Friday, April 24, before the interventions of Saturday, Monday, and Tuesday were even delivered (Hebblethwaite 1998c, 599; Fox 1998a, 13). Some delegates questioned whether the entire synodal proceeding had been prescripted (Fox 1998a, 13). Other delegates noted that while the key themes that the synod delegates brought up repeatedly in their interventions were autonomy, inculturation, and interreligious dialogue, the key themes coming out of the Roman Curia were the uniqueness of Christ and the urgency of evangelization (Hebblethwaite 1998c, 599). Not surprisingly, this *relatio* mirrored much of the curial concerns, as can be seen in its focus on and explication of its three principal themes: (1) God's offer of salvation through his Son Jesus Christ and the Holy Spirit in the context of Asian reality, (2) the evangelizing mission of the church in Asia, and (3) the church's mission of love and service in Asia.

On the one hand, several questions at the end of the *Relatio post disceptationem* drew much criticism from many of the synod delegates for their negative tone and articulation of issues that were never raised at all during the interventions. An example of such a question is this: "How can the Church deal with some unorthodox trends among some theologians with regard to the divinity of Jesus and his unique mediation of salvation?" Another question was framed as a didactic statement: "There is a separation of the mission of Jesus Christ and that of the Holy Spirit. This dichotomy has led to a one-sided appreciation of the work of the Holy Spirit in cultures and religions without affirming the need to proclaim Jesus Christ as the saviour. It might be worthwhile to reflect on this point" (Hebblethwaite 1998c, 599; Fox 1998e). On the other hand, there were some redeeming elements in the *Relatio post disceptationem*—for example, a positive presentation of Jesus as "the guru, the liberator, and the wisdom of God," as manifesting "the feminine or maternal all-embracing love of God," as "the Enlightened One," and as "the one who shares the *kenosis* (or self-emptying) of the Asian peoples" (Hebblethwaite 1998c, 599).

The synod delegates gathered in their eleven small groups to discuss the questions in the *Relatio post disceptationem*. Many of the English-speaking groups were highly critical of the acerbic tone of it. For example, English group H commented rather cynically that "many of the Asian traits which were found in the interventions are lost in the *Relatio post disceptationem*" (Hebblethwaite 1998c, 600). By contrast, the Italian group thought that the *relatio* did not go far enough to reiterate the need for theological orthodoxy. This group asserted that more could be said about the sacraments, the need to emphasize that "the Church must proclaim the Gospel in Asia more firmly," and also the need to "beware of some theologians, especially the Indian ones, who have too strongly emphasised the salvific value of other religions" (Hebblethwaite 1998c, 600). One synod participant remarked that the Italian group "tended to sound more curial" because it had more curial members than the French and English groups (Fox 1998e). The fruits of these small group discussions formed the basis for Cardinal Paul Shan and his committee to formulate a "Unified List of Propositions" comprising fifty-two draft propositions for debate and voting by the synod fathers.

The third and fourth weeks of the synodal proceedings coalesced around two major tasks. First, the synod had to finalize the *sub secreto* propositions that would form the basis for Pope John Paul II to write his apostolic exhortation. Second, the synod had to agree on the text of its final message (*nuntius*) for public dissemination. Many Indonesian and Japanese bishops complained that their propositions were excluded from the list of fifty-two draft propositions, others complained that propositions dealing with "subsidiarity" were rejected, while still others noted that these draft propositions were abstract and nondescript, without any direct relation to Asia at all (Fox 1998c). After much debate and amendments, a final list of fifty-nine *sub secreto* propositions was presented for voting. Although the final list contained fifty-nine, it was actually sixty-one because two of them comprised two parts, each of which was voted on separately. Only the 168 synod fathers were allowed to vote, and they could only vote in terms of "placet" or "non placet." None of the secret propositions received fewer than 140 out of the maximum of 168 votes (Hebblethwaite 1998b). Most of them were passed overwhelmingly or with little opposition or abstention, with the exception of two that elicited strong minority opposition. Proposition 43, which asked for more local church autonomy to achieve inculturation, received fourteen "non placet" votes. Proposition 50, which asked for the enforcement of legitimate canons allowing the Oriental churches more freedom and autonomy in self-governance, drew eleven "non placet" votes (Fox 1998d). Finally, the synod approved its final message on May 13, affirming the church's wish to collaborate with all Asians to improve the quality of life and to share its faith among all while at the same time respecting their religious beliefs and freedom of conscience (UCAN 1998b).

The synod drew to a close on May 14, 1998, with the closing Eucharist at Saint Peter's Basilica. While the liturgy was mainly in Latin, there were distinctive Asian liturgical elements (Hebblethwaite 1998b; UCAN 1998c). The Gospel Acclamation was sung in Tamil according to the Syro-Malankara liturgical ritual, and the gospel was proclaimed in Malayalam according to the Syro-Malabar liturgical ritual. The General Intercessions were offered in Mandarin, Hindi, Japanese, Malay, Tagalog, and Thai. At the preparation of gifts, the eucharistic gifts were presented by Korean women in beautiful traditional costumes and accompanied by a "Condo" dance from Indonesia. The cover of the worship program was again illustrated with Chinese paintings from the Catholic University of Peking. In his homily, Pope John Paul II thanked all the delegates for their endeavors and challenged the Asian church to continue its "mission of love and service" and "remain faithful to the love of Christ" so that they would go and bear fruit that will last (UCAN 1998c).

The Papal Response: Ecclesia in Asia

In his apostolic exhortation *Ecclesia in Asia* (EA), marking the conclusion of the Asian Synod, after explaining that he personally chose the synod's theme—"Jesus Christ the Saviour and His Mission of Love and Service in Asia: '. . . That They May Have Life, and Have It Abundantly'"—Pope John Paul II proceeds to unpack how he understands the synod's theme and express his vision for the new evangelization around the world generally and in Asia in particular, which he first introduced in his apostolic letter *Tertio millennio adveniente* (EA 2, in Phan 2002, 287). After bringing up the fact that Jesus's origins were in Asia, the pope states, quoting from his message to the sixth FABC Plenary Assembly, "Just as in the first millennium the Cross was planted on the soil of Europe, and in the second on that of the Americas and Africa, we can pray that in the Third Christian Millennium a great harvest of faith will be reaped in this vast and vital continent" (EA 1, in Phan 2002, 286). The pope is confident of the "character, spiritual fire and zeal which will assuredly make Asia the land of a bountiful harvest in the coming millennium" (EA 4, in Phan 2002, 288) and is emphatic on the need to commit more resources to the "harvest of souls" in an Asia that he perceives as "ready and plentiful" (EA 9, in Phan 2002, 294).

Many positive aspects of EA are easy to overlook in the midst of its more provocative statements. For example, Pope John Paul II focuses on the concrete realities of modern-day Asia—including historical, cultural, religious, sociopolitical, and economic realities—in chapter 1 of EA (EA 5–9, in Phan 2002, 289–94), explaining that a "critical awareness of the diverse and complex realities of Asia is essential if the people of God on the continent [of Asia] are to respond to God's will for them in the new evangelization" of Asia (EA 5, in Phan 2002, 289). The pope also acknowledges the concerns of many Asian Catholic bishops on the difficulties of proclaiming Jesus as the only savior, which "is fraught with philosophical, cultural and theological difficulties, especially in light of the beliefs of Asia's great religions, deeply intertwined with cultural values and specific world views" (EA 20, in Phan 2002, 303). On this issue, the pontiff recognizes the "pressing need of the local Churches in Asia to present the mystery of Christ to their peoples according to their cultural patterns and ways of thinking" in response to the sensibilities of the Asian peoples (EA 20, in Phan 2002, 305) and proposes a "step-by-step" pedagogy with a preference for "narrative methods akin to Asian cultural forms" and "an evocative pedagogy, using stories, parables, and symbols so characteristic of Asian methodology in teaching" (EA 20, in Phan 2002, 304).

While insisting on the necessity of proclaiming ontological notions about the uniqueness and necessity of Jesus Christ for the salvation of humanity because "they are part of the heritage of faith that must be appropriated and shared again and again in the encounter with the various cultures," Pope John Paul II nevertheless also accepts that in Asia, these ontological notions "can be complemented by more relational, historical and even cosmic perspectives" (EA 20, in Phan 2002, 304). He explains that the church must "be open to new and surprising ways in which the face of Jesus might be presented in Asia," including, for example, Jesus as the teacher of wisdom, the healer, the liberator, the spiritual guide, the enlightened one, the compassionate friend of the poor, the good Samaritan, the good shepherd, the obedient one, the "Incarnate Wisdom of God whose grace brings to fruition the 'seeds' of divine Wisdom already present in the lives, religions and peoples of Asia," and "the Savior 'who can provide meaning to those undergoing unexplainable pain and suffering'" (EA 20, in Phan 2002, in Phan 2002, 304). In addition, he extols the insights and endeavors of missionaries such as Giovanni da Montecorvino, Matteo Ricci, and Roberto de Nobili, urging that their examples be emulated today (EA 20, in Phan 2002, 305).

At times, Pope John Paul II agrees with the FABC on common concerns. For example, the pope echoes the need for a spirituality of prayer and contemplation in Asia, reiterating the point that the FABC addressed in its second Plenary Assembly, "Prayer—the Life of the Church in Asia," in 1978 (EA 23, in Phan 2002, 307–8). He also appreciates the case for life witness in Asia, which many Asian Catholics bishops have stressed at the Asian Synod, noting the important role that life witness plays "in the Asian context, where people are more persuaded by holiness of life than by intellectual argument," as well as acknowledging that many Asians "put more trust in witnesses than in teachers, in experience than in teaching, and in life and action than in theories" (EA 42, in Phan 2002, 323). Clearly, the pope has taken to heart several of the many suggestions that the Asian Catholic bishops made in their synod interventions.

Despite these positive overtures to FABC, what really stands out in EA is the extent to which Pope John Paul II adopts a diametrically opposite position to the FABC on the issues of religious pluralism and engagement with the great religions of Asia through dialogue in postcolonial Asia. In contrast to the FABC, which speaks of the "great religious traditions of our peoples" as "significant and positive elements in the economy of God's design and salvation" (FABC I, 12, 14, in Rosales and Arévalo 1992, 14), the pope makes it clear that he views the soteriological challenges from the Asian religions such as Buddhism and Hinduism as pressing issues and the biggest stumbling blocks to Christianity's growth in Asia, reiterating what he wrote earlier in his apostolic letter *Tertio millennio adveniente* (EA 2, in Phan 2002, 287). Hence while it is true that the pontiff speaks highly of Asian religions and their positive influence on Asians in EA, he nonetheless views these religions and their soteriological elements through a fulfillment matrix, arguing that these religions teach values that "await their fulfillment in Jesus Christ" (EA 6, in Phan 2002, 290). Moreover, the pope is confident that the soteriologies that these Asian religions offer are ultimately inadequate, asserting that only in Jesus do "the peoples of Asia find their deepest questions answered, their hopes fulfilled, their dignity uplifted and their despair conquered" (EA 14, in Phan 2002, 299).

In discussing the relationship between the Holy Spirit, Asian religions, and religious pluralism in EA, Pope John Paul II responds to the FABC's expansive understanding of the Holy Spirit as "active outside the bounds of the visible church" (Bishops' Institute for Interreligious Affairs [BIRA] II, 12, in Rosales and Arévalo 1992, 115) and "at work in all religious traditions" (BIRA IV/12, 7, in Rosales and Arévalo 1992, 326) by declaring that the Holy Spirit "is not an alternative to Christ" but rather "serves as a preparation for the gospel and can only be understood in reference to Christ," in whom "creation and history are redeemed and fulfilled" (EA 16, in Phan 2002, 300–301). The pope restates the point he previously made in *Redemptoris missio* (RM) that there are no two parallel economies of salvation. He argues that the "universal presence of the Holy Spirit therefore cannot serve as an excuse for a failure to proclaim Jesus Christ explicitly as the one and only Savior" because "the universal presence of the Holy Spirit is inseparable from universal salvation in Jesus" (EA 16, in Phan 2002, 301).

More importantly, Pope John Paul II struggles to grasp the implications of the legacy of European colonialism in Asia and many Asians' continuing perceptions of Jesus and the church as a colonial import and therefore foreign to postcolonial Asia, revealing the limits of his ability to understand the full implications of the social, political, and religious impact of ongoing efforts at decolonization across the various regions of postcolonial Asia (EA 9, in Phan 2002, 293). He expresses his frustration at the paradox that Jesus, who was "born on Asia soil," continues to be perceived "as a Western rather than an Asian figure" and therefore foreign to Asia (EA 20, in Phan 2002, 304). He insists that the clear and unequivocal proclamation of the uniqueness and necessity of Jesus Christ for the salvation of humanity is nonnegotiable, repeating a point that he previously made in his encyclical on mission and evangelization, RM (EA 14, in Phan 2002, 298). In his own words, "Jesus is the *one universal mediator*. Even for those who do not explicitly profess faith in him as the Savior, salvation comes as a grace from Jesus Christ through the communication of the Holy Spirit. We believe that Jesus Christ, true God and true man, is the *one Savior* because he *alone*—the Son—accomplished the Father's universal plan of salvation. As the definitive manifestation of the mystery of the Father's love for all, Jesus is indeed *unique*, and it is *precisely this uniqueness of Christ which gives him an absolute and universal significance*" (EA 14, in Phan 2002, 298–99; emphasis added).

Clearly, Pope John Paul II is unyielding in his insistence on the need for proclaiming Christ and his role in the salvation of humanity in all evangelizing work (EA 19, in Phan 2002, 302). For this purpose, the pope outlines a twofold understanding of proclamation in EA. First, he assures Asians that this insistence on proclamation is "prompted not by sectarian impulse nor the spirit of proselytism nor any sense of superiority" but "in obedience to Christ's command, in the knowledge that every person has the right to hear the good news of the God who reveals and gives himself in Christ" (EA 20, in Phan 2002, 303). Second, he contends that respect and esteem for the "rich array of cultures and religions in Asia" and "the complexity of the questions raised" by religious pluralism should not cause the Asian church "to withhold from these non-Christians the proclamation of Jesus Christ" (EA 20, in Phan 2002, 303). Moreover, the pontiff expresses concern at what he perceives to be unwarranted compromises in downplaying certain soteriological claims concerning Jesus in Asia, insisting that "in all evangelizing work, however, it is *the complete truth of Jesus Christ* that must be proclaimed" in order to protect "the integrity of the faith" (EA 23, in Phan 2002, 308; emphasis added). This includes the proclamation that Jesus is the fulfillment of the existential quest of the Asian peoples (see EA 14, in Phan 2002, 299). As far as the pope is concerned, "the question is not whether the Church has something essential to say to the men and women of our time, but how she can say it clearly and convincingly" (EA 29, in Phan 2002, 313).

As for the praxis of dialogue, Pope John Paul II perceives dialogue as *preparatio evangelica*, which leads to the proclamation of the fullness of salvation in Christ alone. For the pope, it is "evangelization in dialogue and dialogue for evangelization" (EA 31, in Phan 2002, 315). On the one hand, Pope John Paul II agrees with the FABC on "the importance of dialogue as a characteristic mode of the Church's life in Asia" (EA 3, in Phan 2002, 288), perceiving that dialogue "is not simply a strategy for peaceful coexistence among peoples; it is an essential part of the Church's mission" (EA 29, in Phan 2002, 314); it is "more than a way of fostering mutual knowledge and enrichment; it is a part of the Church's evangelizing mission, an expression of the mission *ad gentes*" (EA 31, in Phan 2002, 315). On the other hand, the pope is adamant that "Christians bring to interreligious dialogue the firm belief that the fullness of salvation comes from Christ alone and that the Church community to which they belong is the ordinary means of salvation" because "although the Church gladly acknowledges whatever is true and holy" in Asian religions, this "does not lessen her duty and resolve to proclaim without failing Jesus Christ who is 'the way and the truth and the life'" (EA 31, in Phan 2002, 315). As far as the pontiff was concerned, "the fact that the followers of other religions can receive God's grace and be saved by Christ apart from the ordinary means which he has established does not thereby cancel the call to faith and baptism which God wills for all people" (EA 31, in Phan 2002, 315).

Responding to EA

The FABC's response to Pope John Paul II's EA was conveyed first through the response of Indonesian cardinal Julius Riyadi Darmaatmadja, the president delegate of the synod for Asia, in his closing remarks in Sacred Heart Cathedral (a.k.a. Delhi Cathedral; Darmaatmadja 1999) and second in the final statement of the seventh FABC Plenary Assembly (Eilers 2002, 1–16). The initial response of the FABC to EA, as presented by Cardinal Darmaatmadja, reveals a careful nuancing of Pope John Paul II's strong stance in EA, setting the stage for the seventh FABC Plenary Assembly to present its own measured response to EA.

Cardinal Julius Riyadi Darmaatmadja

In his response to EA, Cardinal Darmaatmadja begins by acknowledging Pope John Paul II's push for a "new evangelization" in Asia (see EA 2 and 5, in Phan 2002, 287, 289), as well as the pope's insistence on the necessity of the proclamation of Jesus and his gospel in Asia (EA 14, in Phan 2002, 298). Referring to the pope's vision of new evangelization in Asia, he explains that such a proclamation should proceed not on the basis that Jesus is not yet present in the Asian world but rather because "we can find Jesus present in the world" because "he has always been present and working in the world, including the world of Asia" (Darmaatmadja 1999, 888). While Pope John Paul II begins from the position that the church has something to offer to the Asian peoples, who should not be denied the opportunity to receive what the church has to give, Cardinal Darmaatmadja points out that for the "new evangelization" in Asia to be successful, the Asian church needs to be aware of and respond to the existential questions and longings of the Asian peoples rather than presuming to know what the Asian peoples are looking for and imposing its own answers. In making the discernment of the deepest inner aspirations of the Asian peoples as the starting point of mission and evangelization, Cardinal Darmaatmadja is referencing proposition 3 of the Asian Synod, which states that "the Churches must be immersed in the diverse contrasting and even conflicting realities of Asia. Only such immersion will help the Church define her mission to the people of Asia in an intelligible and acceptable manner" (quoted in Darmaatmadja 1999, 889).

On the one hand, Cardinal Darmaatmadja reiterates the importance for the Asian church to be "fully and deeply present in the one Church of Christ shepherded by the Pope as the unifying factor." On the other hand, he points out that the Asian church has to be "at the same time deeper and deeper rooted in our own cultures and our deepest inner aspirations as peoples of Asia" (Darmaatmadja 1999, 888). This entails a solidarity with the Asian peoples and their existential concerns and deepest aspirations, a "new way of being Church" that "is expected to become in a concrete way a Church 'with' and 'for' the people in order to achieve their integral human development, culminating in the fullness of life given by Our Lord Jesus Christ" (890).

More importantly, although Cardinal Darmaatmadja uses Pope John Paul II's preferred term of *new evangelization*, he carefully nuances it by explaining that in the contemporary postcolonial Asian context, "new evangelization means . . . bringing the Good News into all dimensions of making it anew . . . a new life in a real commitment of people and groups of people with each other and with God. . . . It is the fullness of the Reign of God that Jesus proclaimed and that we are to proclaim in our respective contexts." As he puts it, "Our new evangelization should, on the one hand, reveal the all-transforming power of the Spirit of the resurrected Jesus Christ. It should, on the other hand, speak about justice, peace, and the wholeness of creation as fruits and signs of God's eschatological realm" (Darmaatmadja 1999, 890). An astute observer would notice how Cardinal Darmaatmadja carefully shifts the attention away from Pope John Paul II's emphasis on proclaiming Jesus Christ as the savior of the world in favor of the FABC's regnocentric theology of mission as discussed in chapter 4 of this book. More importantly, he contends that in the postcolonial Asian realities, proclamation per se does not suffice:

> Yes, it is true that there is no authentic evangelization
> without announcing Jesus Christ, Saviour of the whole
> human race. *But for Asia, there will be no complete
> evangelization unless there is dialogue with other religions
> and cultures.* There is no full evangelization *if there is no
> answer to the deep yearnings of the peoples of Asia.* There
> is no convincing and trustworthy announcement of Jesus
> as the Saviour, unless along with, or even preceding this
> announcing, *the Church presents the actual loving ministry
> of Jesus which rescues people from situations of injustice,*

persecution, misery, and in the place of these brings life,
yes, even life in abundance. (Darmaatmadja 1999, 891;
emphasis added)

On the one hand, Cardinal Darmaatmadja agrees with Pope John Paul II that "Jesus is often perceived as foreign to Asia" (EA 20, in Phan 2002, 304). On the other hand, while the pontiff proposes a "pedagogy which will introduce people step by step to the full appropriation of the mystery," the cardinal observes that the real problem is the church's alienation from the postcolonial Asian realities by its foreignness. Hence he suggests that the church immerses itself in the postcolonial Asian milieu in order to "help the Church define her mission to the people of Asia in an intelligible and acceptable manner" (Darmaatmadja 1999, 889).

On the issue of religious pluralism and the great religions of Asia, which Pope John Paul II perceives as challenges confronting the church's missionary enterprise in Asia (EA 2, in Phan 2002, 287) or otherwise incomplete or inadequate for salvation and awaiting their fulfillment in Christ (EA 6, in Phan 2002, 290), Cardinal Darmaatmadja is emphatic that Asian religions are not rivals. Instead, he asserts that they "need to be considered specifically as partners in dialogue" (Darmaatmadja 1999, 888). While Pope John Paul II draws attention away from the Holy Spirit to focus on Jesus Christ (EA 16, in Phan 2002, 301), Cardinal Darmaatmadja reiterates the FABC's theology of the Holy Spirit at work within Asian cultures and religions: "Religious and cultural aspects which bear values of universal goodness and truth, fittingly, are to be accepted as treasures, since they approximate the marks of the guidance of the Holy Spirit who has been working within these cultures and living human institutions (Cf. RM no. 28). In the eyes of religious adherents and practitioners of such values, the new way the Church bears itself will enable these people to understand us better, enable them to come closer to us, but *also enrich us in return in the way we live our christian lives*" (Darmaatmadja 1999, 888–89; emphasis added).

Cardinal Darmaatmadja also takes the opportunity to bring to the forefront two synodal propositions that were not mentioned by Pope John Paul II in EA: "Our theologians deserve to be suitably supported so as to delve into these themes in a manner that is at once serious and courageous but also faithful to Sacred Scripture and the Church Tradition (Cf. Prop. 7). In matters that involve inculturation of such a nature, 'Local Bishops' Conferences' should be fittingly granted a more significant role in decision making (Cf. Prop. 36)" (Darmaatmadja 1999, 889). Clearly, Cardinal Darmaatmadja perceives inculturation as "immersion" in Asian realities such that the gospel and the church take on a truly Asian face, in contrast to Pope John Paul II's understanding of cultures as *ancillae theologiae*, "to be used as pedagogical vehicles to evangelize Asians" (EA 20, in Phan 2002, 304).

FABC VII: A Renewed Church in Asia on a Mission of Love and Service

Less than two months after Pope John Paul II presented his apostolic exhortation, EA, the seventh Plenary Assembly of the FABC met in Samphran, Thailand, from January 3 to 12, 2000. The official theme of FABC VII ("A Renewed Church in Asia on a Mission of Love and Service") was based on the official theme of the Asian Synod—"Jesus Christ the Saviour and His Mission of Love and Service in Asia: '... That They May Have Life, and Have It Abundantly'"—with a crucial difference. Unlike the official theme of the Asian Synod, there is no reference to "Jesus Christ the Saviour" in the official theme of FABC VII.

When one compares the FABC's response to EA in the final statement of FABC VII, one is struck by the extent to which the FABC seeks to nuance EA critically and carefully. For example,

rather than simply adopting Pope John Paul II's preferred terminology of *new evangelization*, the FABC coins a new term—*active
integral evangelization* (Eilers 2002, 3)—to define an intersectional approach to doing Christian mission in postcolonial Asia that
integrates life witness, intercultural and interreligious dialogue,
and social justice. The final statement of FABC VII explains the
rationale for this term as follows:

> For thirty years, as we have tried to reformulate our
> Christian identity in Asia, we have addressed different
> issues, one after another: evangelization, inculturation,
> dialogue, the Asian-ness of the Church, justice, the option
> for the poor, etc. Today, after three decades, we no longer
> speak of such distinct issues. We are addressing present
> needs that are massive and increasingly complex. *These
> issues are not separate topics to be discussed, but aspects
> of an integrated approach to our Mission of Love and
> Service. We need to feel and act "integrally." As we face
> the needs of the 21st century, we do so with Asian hearts,
> in solidarity with the poor and the marginalized, in union
> with all our Christian brothers and sisters, and by joining
> hands with all men and women of Asia of many different
> faiths. Inculturation, dialogue, justice and the option for
> the poor are aspects of whatever we do.* (Eilers 2002, 8;
> emphasis added)

Referring to the issue of Pope John Paul II's insistence on the
necessity of proclaiming Jesus Christ for the salvation of humanity,
the FABC deftly nuances it by linking proclamation to life witness
in solidarity and empathy with the Asian peoples in the fullness of
their cultures, religions, and daily lived experiences. To this end,
FABC VII testifies to the need for life witness in postcolonial Asia as
follows: "The most effective means of evangelization and service

in the name of Christ has always been and continues to be the *witness of life*. The embodiment of our faith in sharing and compassion (sacrament) supports the credibility of our obedience to the Word (proclamation). This witnessing has to become the way of the Gospel for persons, institutions and the whole Church community. *Asian people will recognize the Gospel that we announce when they see in our life the transparency of the message of Jesus and the inspiring and healing figure of men and women immersed in God"* (Eilers 2002, 12–13; emphasis added).

Unlike Pope John Paul II, who reduces Asian cultural and religious traditions to mere pedagogical tools for proclaiming the gospel in Asia, FABC VII is adamant that the Asian church has to immerse itself in and embrace these cultural and religious traditions in an effort to become truly Asian, as well as to empathize and be in solidarity with the Asian peoples in the fullness of their lived realities, a point that Cardinal Darmaatmadja also made earlier on behalf of the FABC at the pope's presentation of EA in Delhi. On this issue, FABC VII makes the following powerful statement:

We are committed to *the emergence of the Asianness of the Church in Asia*. This means that *the Church has to be an embodiment of the Asian vision and values of life*, especially interiority, harmony, a holistic and inclusive approach to every area of life. . . . This is important, because *our contacts with those of other religious traditions have to be at the level of depth*, rather than just the level of ideas or action. We are aware that this Asianness, founded on solid values, is a special gift the world is awaiting. For the whole world is in need of a holistic paradigm for meeting the challenges of life. In this task, together with all Asians, the Church, a tiny minority in this vast continent, has a singular contribution to make, and this contribution is the task of the whole Church in Asia. (Eilers 2002, 8–9; emphasis added)

In making this statement, FABC VII cites EA 6 with approval, highlighting "the innate spiritual insight and moral wisdom in the Asian soul" as well as the "growing sense of 'being Asian,'" which "is best discovered and affirmed not in confrontation and opposition, but in the spirit of complementarity and harmony," enabling the Asian church to "communicate the Gospel in a way which is faithful both to her own Tradition and to the Asian Soul" (Eilers 2002, 9).

Finally, while Pope John Paul II spoke of Jesus as the door that leads to life and salvation in his speech at Delhi Cathedral on the promulgation of EA (John Paul II 1999, 400), the seventh Plenary Assembly uses the imagery of "doors" to highlight the fact that mission in postcolonial Asia is about going through the doors of the Asian church "out into the world of the peoples of Asia and into their struggles and joys, which are also ours" (Eilers 2002, 15).

The Legacy of the Asian Synod

Many experienced synod-watchers have pointed out that the Asian Synod stood apart from the other synods by the public and candid discussion of contentious issues in front of Pope John Paul II and the curial bureaucracy (Fox 1998a, 13). Indeed, Pope John Paul II and his curial officials were present and heard the many frank speeches by the various Asian bishops and other delegates directly during the synod proceedings. Without a doubt, the Asian bishops, Eastern and Latin Catholic alike, knew what they wanted from Rome, which they made clear in their interventions on the synod floor. For example, both the Eastern Catholic and the Latin Catholic bishops were united in their request for more trust from Rome and more autonomy in matters of ecclesial organization, administration, and liturgical practices in their local churches. For the Eastern Catholic bishops, it was also the retrieval of their ancient ecclesial heritage of autocephaly, while the Latin Catholic bishops wanted more autonomy in matters of inculturation, interreligious dialogue, and shaping a distinctively Asian way of doing Christian mission in the diverse and pluralistic realities of postcolonial Asia.

Commenting on this candor and outspokenness by the Asian bishops, an unnamed European journalist based in Rome remarks that "the Americans knew what couldn't be said and censored themselves. They ended up hedging their thoughts. This time the bishops are speaking their minds" (quoted in Fox 1998a, 13). One synod participant—Cardinal Luis A. "Chito" Tagle, who is a Filipino theologian, the former archbishop of Manila, and now the prefect of the Congregation for the Evangelization of Peoples—comments, "In comparison to the delegates of the two previous synods [for Africa and the Americas], the delegates to the Asian Synod were bolder, more courageous. They said what they wanted to say in front of the Holy Father! A Latin American Cardinal told me, 'I thought you Asians are serene, peace-loving, and quiet. Why are the bishops talking that way?'" (1998, 371–72).

More significantly, the Asian Synod marks an important milestone in the history and achievements of the FABC. Peter C. Phan describes it as "the coming of age of the Asian Catholic Church" that "shows how far the Asian Catholic Church has moved forward" in terms of its reception of Vatican II and contributions to the council's goals and trajectories (2018, 14). It is instructive that the Asian bishops, representing the Eastern Catholic and the Latin Catholic churches across the different regions of Asia, came well prepared to the Asian Synod as a result of their own experiences of collaboration and consultation among themselves under the aegis of the CPCO and FABC, respectively. One could say that the spirit of episcopal collegiality, consultation, and collaboration, which has always been present within existing supranational collegial networks such as the CPCO and FABC, has enabled the Asian bishops of the Eastern Catholic and the Latin Catholic churches to collaborate and work together on shared issues, goals, and objectives.

6

Looking Ahead: Challenges and Possibilities

In the preceding chapters, we explored the foundational aspects of the Federation of Asian Bishops' Conferences' (FABC's) new ways of doing intersectional theologizing, being church, and witnessing to Jesus, the gospel, and the Reign of God in solidarity and empathy with the Asian peoples within the fullness of their cultures, religions, and subaltern socioeconomic challenges as well as amid the diverse intercultural and plurireligious realities of postcolonial Asia. In this chapter, we will examine the unresolved challenges and new possibilities for the FABC in the contemporary Asian realities, focusing on how the FABC maps out the social and virtual geographies of transnational Asian Christianities, especially when we talk about going beyond the boundaries and borders of being church that are established by Eurocentric theologizing. What if the FABC could reimagine an Asian Christianity and an Asian church for the future? What would that look like?

For the purposes of our investigation, we will examine the contemporary theological issues and opportunities emerging from two case studies of migration and insider movements, evaluating their implications for rethinking the contours of Asian Christianity, theologizing in postcolonial Asia, being church, and doing Christian mission. How does the FABC respond to the developments in the daily lived experiences of Asian Christians who are on the move across Asia and beyond, in online and virtual communities, and in insider movements, which comprise Asians who choose to follow Jesus while deciding to remain within their own cultural and religious traditions? Underlying both case studies is the understanding that the future of Asian Christianity and being church in postcolonial Asia hinges on migration and insider movements, both of which challenge how we understand church structures and membership, community belonging and participation, and their implications for shaping postcolonial Asian theologizing.

Migration in Asia

To say that we are currently living in an age of massive movements and displacements of peoples all across Asia is an understatement. According to the International Organization for Migration's (IOM's) *World Migration Report 2011*, about one billion people (or one in seven of the world's population) are migrants (IOM 2011, 49). The report also notes that five of the top ten emigration countries are located in Asia—India (2), China (4), Bangladesh (6), Pakistan (7), and the Philippines (9; 2011, 68, citing World Bank 2011, 3).

On the one hand, the phenomenon of migration in Asia has a long, varied, and complex history stretching back thousands of years. Beginning with the nomadic tribes that wandered the vast expanse of the Asian continent in search of water and grazing lands, the caravans of traders and missionaries who traveled on the Silk Road across vast stretches of Asia, and the invading armies of big Asian empires that displaced peoples and communities from their ancestral lands, migration has always defined the Asian continent in every age. On the other hand, the twenty-first century is witnessing the tremendous growth of massive internal displacements of peoples from rural to urban centers in a quest for better opportunities for success, as well as huge external movements of peoples from those Asian countries who are either economically struggling or caught up in political, religious, or social strife, seeking to start new lives and pursue their dreams and hopes elsewhere across Asia.

Without a doubt, migration defines much of the contemporary postcolonial Asian landscape. In reality, a significant number of Asians are migrants, whether internal or external, willingly or unwillingly, permanent or transient. Voluntary migrations may be internal—for example, the hordes of Chinese and Indians leaving their rural provinces in search of work in the booming coastal regions and big cities of China and India—or external, as exemplified by the many Filipinos, Indonesians, Indians, Bangladeshis, Chinese, and others who pursue better opportunities outside their homelands as doctors, nurses, engineers, seafarers, construction workers, domestic helpers, and factory workers in the wealthier regions of Asia, including the Persian Gulf States of the Arabian Peninsula, Hong Kong, Japan, Taiwan, and Singapore. These voluntary migrants can seek to be either permanent residents or citizens of their adopted countries or remain as transient migrants, who are always on the move for better opportunities and not intending to stay in any one particular place permanently. Involuntary migrants include not just those refugees who are fleeing wars and social strife, economic upheavals, political instabilities, and religious tensions and persecutions but also the many economic migrants, especially vulnerable women and children, who are exploited and trafficked by underworld gangs, smuggling networks, and secret societies for cheap labor and sex trafficking. The sheer violence and abject dehumanization that many of these women and children experience reveal the dark underbelly of migration and call for a global response and concerted effort on an international scale to resolve these challenges. In any event, migration—whether voluntary or involuntary, internal or external, permanent or transient—arises from the transnational push and pull of global economic supply and demand forces that are driven by immense poverty, extreme socioeconomic imbalances, violent ethnic and religious strife, and the insatiable demand for cheap human labor.

Migration in the FABC Documents

In the early years of its existence, the FABC merely dealt with the issue of migration and its challenges tangentially in its statements and documents, making minor references to migrants in the *Syllabus of "Mission Concerns"* of the Bishops' Institute for Missionary Apostolate (BIMA) III (1982) and the final statement of BIMA IV (1988). Specifically, article 11 of BIMA III's *Syllabus of "Mission Concerns"* states that the "pastoral care for the great number of Asians who have emigrated from their homelands for economic reasons demands the serious missionary concern of the churches" (Rosales and Arévalo 1992, 108). BIMA IV encourages the bishops to use "the mobility and migration of the faithful as an opportunity to spread the Gospel of Christ" and "inspire, educate, and organize... migrants to be witnesses of Christ wherever they may go" (Rosales and Arévalo 1992, 294). In the absence of any formal statement from the FABC during this period, several episcopal conferences in Asia released their own statements on migration—for example, the Philippines in 1988, Taiwan in 1989, and Japan in 1993 (Battistella 1995).

In its subsequent statements and documents, which we will examine in greater detail below, we see that the FABC seeks to undergird its theology and praxis of migration in a "commitment and service to life" within the diversity and plurality of postcolonial Asia, which we discussed earlier in chapter 3. We will explore how the FABC's "commitment and service to life" in empathy and solidarity with the masses of peoples who are on the move across Asia are demonstrated in its call to the Asian church to walk together with and accompany these migrants as well as respond to the pathos and struggles that they experience in their daily lives, including poverty, economic marginalization, and racial, political, and religious tensions. As far as the FABC is concerned, migration cannot be separated from the complex interplay of social, economic, class, religious, and political factors that interact to displace peoples from their homelands. Whether voluntary or forced, migration reveals the vulnerability, insecurity, uncertainty, and humiliation of millions of Asians who find themselves on the move, either internally or beyond their national borders, as they deal with survival, uprootedness, and exploitation in their quest for a better life for themselves and their families.

FABC V: Journeying Together toward the Third Millennium (1990)

The major turning point came with the fifth FABC Plenary Assembly, which highlights the injustice that is experienced by migrants, both voluntary and involuntary, in its final statement: "We are deeply conscious, therefore, that within our context of change there is the unchanging reality of injustice. There remains in Asia massive poverty.... Poverty likewise drives both men and women to become migrant workers, often destroying family life in the process. Political conflict and economic desperation have driven millions to become refugees, to living for years in camps that are sometimes in effect crowded prisons" (FABC V, 2.2.1, in Rosales and Arévalo 1992, 276–77). Responding to this problem, FABC V asserts that Asian Christians "must live in *companionship*, as true *partners* with all Asians as they pray, work, struggle and suffer for a better human life, and as they search for the meaning of human life and progress" (FABC V, 6.2, in Rosales and Arévalo 1992, 283). FABC V also insists that Asian Christians must walk in solidarity with the "exploited women and workers, unwelcome refugees, victims of violations of human rights," seeking to "denounce, in deeds, if it is not possible to do so in words, the injustices, oppressions, exploitations, and inequalities resulting in so much of the suffering that is evident in the Asian situation" (FABC V, 6.4, in Rosales and Arévalo 1992, 283–84).

Journeying Together in Faith with the Filipino Migrant Workers in Asia (1993)

As a follow-up to FABC V, the FABC Office of Human Development continued the discussion by organizing a symposium on Filipino migrant workers in Asia, which was held in Hong Kong in 1993 and attended by delegates of the episcopal conferences and diocesan commissions in Japan, South Korea, Taiwan, Hong Kong, Macau, Singapore, Thailand, Malaysia, and the Philippines. The final statement of this symposium, entitled *Journeying Together in Faith with the Filipino Migrant Workers in Asia*, begins with an acknowledgment of the immense contributions of millions of migrant workers from the Philippines to the growing global economy (Eilers 1997, 47). While it observes that migration does have "both positive and negative effects on the country of origin as well as the receiving country" (Eilers 1997, 48–49), it points out those Filipino migrant workers, male and female alike, who often experience serious human rights abuses. For example, Filipino women, who are often employed in the domestic and entertainment sectors, are "frequently submitted to humiliation, harassment and sexual abuse" (Eilers 1997, 50). Filipino men, who make up the single largest national group in the seafarers and fish workers sector, not only "face physical and verbal abuse" but also experience difficulties in claiming compensation for disabilities (Eilers 1997, 50).

Moreover, the symposium participants recognized the consequences of migration for the disintegration of the family unit, with deleterious effects on children and their parents (Eilers 1997, 50). The symposium delegates explored the implications of migration on families and concluded, "There is a very urgent need to take seriously the implications of migration on marriage and family life. The social, spiritual and moral implications need urgent assessment by all. Husbands separated from wives, and children from parents are a direct consequence of contract labor migration, showing signs of breakdown of both marriages and families" (Eilers 1997, 55).

On the theological aspects of migration, the symposium delegates view migration as a reality that not only points to the birth of a new world order based on the growing interdependence among nations but also confirms the fundamental right of every person to migrate freely because "the world belongs to everyone" (Eilers 1997, 51). They emphasize that the Asian church has to "accompany the Migrant as a Human Person, following the example of Christ himself. This journeying of the Church together with the Migrant Worker, is the sign of solidarity within the universal Church and a sharing in the common evangelizing mission entrusted to all the followers of Christ. Growing in faith as a local Church, made up of people of different nationalities is a new sign of unity" (Eilers 1997, 53).

On the one hand, the symposium delegates affirm that migration should not be forced and reiterate that migrants' human rights must be respected and that they should not be subject to inhumane working and living conditions (Eilers 1997, 52). On the other hand, they also urge both the originating and the receiving churches to address the root causes of migration and its negative impact on migrants. Specifically, they emphasize that churches that are receiving migrants ought to welcome and assist them to "relate, participate and integrate themselves to the local Church in the various activities, and at the same time be able to share their faith and cultural heritage with the local Church and people" (Eilers 1997, 53). This is because local receiving churches have the responsibility to protect the rights and promote the dignity of these migrant workers, working "closely with the local Government to make available services to the migrants who are a very important part of the labor force and contribute to the economy and society" (Eilers 1997, 54).

FABC VI: Christian Discipleship in Asia Today—Service to Life (1995)

The sixth Plenary Assembly of the FABC highlights "the insecurity and vulnerability of migrants, refugees, the displaced ethnic and indigenous peoples, and the pain and agonies of exploited workers, especially the child laborers in our countries" (FABC VI, 7, in Eilers 1997, 4). In unequivocal language, it states that solidarity and empathy require "a resolve to work with our Asian sisters and brothers in liberating our societies from whatever oppresses and degrades human life and creation" (FABC VI, 14.2, in Eilers 1997, 8), which includes migrants and their dehumanizing experiences. Specifically, FABC VI describes the plight of migrants as follows: "Special attention is given to the displaced in our societies: political and ecological refugees and migrant workers. They are marginalized and exploited by the system, denied of their place in society and must go elsewhere to seek a dignified life. In welcoming them we expose the causes of their displacement, work toward conditions for a more human living in community, experience the universal dimension of the Kingdom (Gal 3:28) and appreciate new opportunities for evangelization and intercultural dialogue" (FABC VI, 15.5, in Eilers 1997, 11).

Colloquium on Church in Asia in the 21st Century (1997)

The issue of migration also came up for discussion at the FABC's Colloquium on Church in Asia in the 21st Century, which was organized by the FABC Office of Human Development. The colloquium participants met in Pattaya City, Thailand, in 1997 to discuss the theme of "Towards a Communion and Solidarity in the Context of Globalization." On the issue of migrants and their challenges, the colloquium participants suggest that dioceses intervene more actively to "take up the cause of migrant workers through the legal process of the host country by providing financial support and lawyers to fight for their rights" (Eilers 2002, 40). The final statement of this colloquium also outlines four practical steps that the FABC could adopt in response to the challenges and needs of migrants and their families. First, it recommends that the migrant commissions of the various episcopal conferences initiate bilateral meetings to discuss and explore solutions to the challenges experienced by migrants. Second, it suggests that formation programs be organized for the training of pastoral workers for migrants. Third, it proposes that diocesan pastoral programs also cater to the pastoral care of the families of migrants. Fourth, it highlights the need to link the issue of migration with the broader issue of human labor (Eilers 2002, 40).

FABC VII: A Renewed Church in Asia on a Mission of Love and Service (2000)

At the seventh Plenary Assembly of the FABC, the Asian Catholic bishops focused, among other things, on the ever-growing migration and refugee movements and called for an urgent and adequate pastoral response to address their dehumanizing plight. In the final statement of FABC VII, we find the following call to action from the FABC:

In the light of the teaching of the Church, we affirm that migration and refugee movements, which result in depersonalization, loss of human dignity and the break up of families, are moral issues confronting the conscience of the Church and that of our Asian nations. As for the Church in Asia, these pose urgent pastoral challenges to evolve life-giving, service-oriented programs of action within the pastoral mission of the Church. The Church should join hands with all who are concerned with the rights of the migrants and their situation, keeping in mind that the migrants themselves are to be the primary agents of change. (FABC VII, 5, in Eilers 2002, 11)

FABC VIII: The Asian Family towards a Culture of Integral Life (2004)

The eighth Plenary Assembly of the FABC continued the approach adopted by FABC VII, focusing in particular on Asian families and the challenges that they experience in their daily life struggles. In particular, FABC VIII identifies the twin forces of globalization and urbanization as accounting for the bulk of contemporary migration patterns in Asia (Eilers 2007, 6). It also highlights the harmful and destructive impact of migration on Asian families: "It is true that salaries [migrants] earn abroad are significantly much more than they can earn in their home countries, but at the price of the stability of their families, the proper education and maturation of their children, who are deprived of the presence, the guidance, and love of both parents at their most formative and impressionable age" (FABC VIII, 15, in Eilers 2007, 6). FABC VIII also warns of the cultural dislocations and breakdown in family and communal ties between these migrants and their families and communities back home (FABC VIII, 16, in Eilers 2007, 7), reiterating that "migrant workers and their families urgently need great pastoral care from the churches of sending and receiving countries" (FABC VIII, 17, in Eilers 2007, 7).

FEISA V: *Pastoral Care of Migrants and Refugees:*
A New Way of Being Church (2002)

Organized by the FABC Office of Human Development, the Faith
Encounters in Social Action (FEISA) seeks to promote interreligious dialogue through social involvement, emphasizing that
the postcolonial Asian church needs to ground its mission and
outreach intersectionally in a threefold dialogue with the Asian
peoples in the fullness of their cultures, religious traditions, and
poverty (Eilers 2007, 89). Meeting in Kota Kinabalu, Malaysia, in
2002 with the theme "'From Distrust to Respect . . . Reject to
Welcome': Study Days on Undocumented Migrants and Refugees,"
FEISA V seeks to draw the close connection between migration,
mission, and engagement with the plurireligious Asian milieu. Its
final statement, entitled *Pastoral Care of Migrants and Refugees:*
A New Way of Being Church, is a thorough discussion on the challenges faced by undocumented migrants and refugees and what
the Asian church could do to respond to these challenges.

FEISA V sees the phenomenon of ongoing migration in Asia
within the broader framework of migration as "part and parcel of
human civilization" (Eilers 2007, 112) and "a natural phenomenon"
that arises from "the inherent right of people to move." At the same
time, the document also acknowledges that not all migrations
are freely and voluntarily undertaken. It contends that the Asian
church has to respond to the dilemma of Asians who migrate in
a quest to ensure their survival because of physical or economic
threats (114). The approach that FEISA V adopts is built on its
understanding that migration "offers the Church all over the world
an opportunity to reach out to the ones most discriminated by
society today. Being in solidarity with them, offers us the opportunity to offer the Good News of the Gospel to them as individuals
and as a community" (128). Underlying its recommendations is
its vision that the Asian church should advocate for the human

dignity and rights of migrants regardless of race, religion, or legal status as part of its wider stance of advocating for the rights and aspirations of the poor and marginalized (Eilers 2007, 128–29). As far as FEISA V is concerned, the "Good News is not only to be preached but it is to be lived and practiced in concrete day-to-day circumstances among people of many faiths" (Eilers 2007, 130).

FEISA V takes as its starting point Pope John Paul II's insistence in his 1996 "Message for World Migration Day on Undocumented Migrants" that "a migrant's irregular legal status cannot allow him/her to lose his/her dignity, since he/she is endowed with inalienable rights, which can neither be violated nor ignored" (Eilers 2007, 111; see also John Paul II 1996). In that 1996 message, Pope John Paul II also made it clear that the church should defend the rights of the undocumented migrants:

> In the Church no one is a stranger, and the Church is not foreign to anyone, anywhere. As a sacrament of unity and thus a sign and a binding force for the whole human race, the Church is the place where illegal immigrants should be recognized and accepted as brothers and sisters.... Solidarity means taking responsibility for those in trouble. For Christians, the migrant is not merely an individual to be respected in accordance with the norms established by law, but a person whose presence challenges them and whose needs become an obligation for their responsibility. "What have you done to your brother?" (cf. Gn 4:9). The answer should not be limited to what is imposed by law, but should be made in the manner of solidarity. (John Paul II 1996)

Taking its cue from Pope John Paul II, FEISA V states that both undocumented migrants and asylum seekers "remain children of God" and "deserve Christian love and protection" to maintain their human dignity, notwithstanding that they often "have no legal right to remain in a given national territory" (Eilers 2007, 111). While FEISA V reiterates the "inalienable dignity and rights of people on the move" and "acknowledges the right of sovereign nation-states to regulate the movement of people across their borders," it is equally insistent that "this right must be exercised at the service of the universal common good" (117). As it explains, "People on the move must not be reduced to instruments of economic or political strategies. All of their human rights must be respected. The freedom of people to move should be preserved and restrictions imposed only where this is necessary in order to protect the common good. People have a right to move in order to seek safety, freedom and a decent level of material welfare" (117).

Hence FEISA V maintains that the Asian church should treat all migrants alike in its pastoral outreach regardless of their status and what their motivations may be for leaving their homelands: "Whatever the reason is, the Church that embodies the mission of Christ cannot remain indifferent to issues relating/affecting people on the move. The Church that is universal both in outlook and in its essence is duty bound to learn from the migrants and at the same time, respond to their needs" (Eilers 2007, 114). It points out that Asian Christians should begin by listening "to people in an irregular situation or in search of asylum, in order to know exactly what their situation is, and also provide them with their basic needs" because "asylum-seekers and migrants in an illegal situation have the right to be provided with the necessary means of subsistence" (115). As it explains, "Christian solidarity simply sees the need to take care of human beings, especially young people, minors and children who are incapable of defending themselves because they lack protection under the law and often do not know the language of the country in which they have been obliged to seek refuge due to natural catastrophes, wars, violence, persecution, even genocide in their own country or due to existing economic conditions such as to endanger their physical integrity or life itself" (115).

FEISA V further contends that the Asian church "seeks to defend the dignity and rights of people on the move regardless of their race, religion and legal status" and, in particular, pay "attention not only to the practical and physical needs, but also to their social, psychological and spiritual needs" (Eilers 2007, 118). Pope Benedict XVI makes a similar point when he calls on Christians "to open their arms and hearts to every person, from whatever nation they come," in his address to the 2006 assembly of the Pontifical Council for the Pastoral Care of Migrants and Itinerant People on the theme of "Migration and Itinerancy from and towards Islamic Majority Countries" (2006).

On the issue of poverty and migration, FEISA V draws attention to the reality of poverty as the force behind much of the mass migrations in Asia—whether internal or external, voluntary or involuntary—and recommends that the Asian church should stand in solidarity with the poor and marginalized (Eilers 2007, 128–29). In this regard, FEISA V recognizes that the problems of migration arise "because of the terrible situation surrounding the migration phenomenon: of injustice, discrimination, violence, violation of rights, inhuman living and working conditions, and fear especially for those who are undocumented, etc." (113).

At the same time, FEISA V sees migration as facilitating opportunities for intercultural and interreligious encounters "because in our globalised world, it gives concrete chances for people of different nationalities, cultures and creeds to come together, know each other and share with one another," thereby removing or at least reducing prejudice and indifference (Eilers 2007, 113). Hence FEISA V goes a step further to insist that in addressing the needs of migrants, the Asian church "must work together with people of other faiths or none," joining "with all people of good will to respond to other sisters and brothers affirming their full humanity and the inalienable rights that arise from their humanity" (118). In particular, it explains the theological basis for this outreach to migrants of other religions in terms of the Asian church's recognition of its own minority status in Asia and seizing the initiative to make positive contributions to interreligious relations: "Making the migrants/refugees the target of our pastoral care is our concrete way of witnessing to the people of Asia. Being a 'little flock' in the midst of other ancient religions/beliefs, the Asian Church cannot remain 'inward looking.' The Good News is not only to be preached but it is to be lived/practised in concrete day-to-day circumstances of many faiths. Thus, efforts to provide pastoral care to migrants have to include inter-religious dimensions. The Church can and should take the initiative. By doing so, we are witnessing to the mission of Christ through our actions" (122–23).

For FEISA V, "interreligious dialogue is imperative" and integral to the Asian church's theology and praxis of migration—that is, the Asian church "dialogues with all regardless of creed, nationality, race, political stance, or other discriminatory factors especially undocumented or documented status of migrant workers" (Eilers 2007, 125). This applies to Asian Christians migrating to non-Christian countries in Asia, as well as non-Christian migrants interacting with Asian Christians.

In the first instance, FEISA V refers to Asian Christians who migrate to non-Christian countries in Asia, pointing out that they can be "living witnesses of Christ through Christian love of the members for one another and for the migrant, both Christian and non-Christian" (Eilers 2007, 113). It encourages Asian Christian migrants "to invite their friends of other religions to the church where they may receive a warm reception" (120). In a similar vein, the Pontifical Council for the Pastoral Care of Migrants and Itinerant People's 2004 instruction, *Erga migrantes caritas Christi*, calls on local churches to welcome; provide pastoral care, assistance, and hospitality to; and seek to integrate migrants within their local communities regardless of their religions (2004, 42). In particular, *Erga migrantes caritas Christi* speaks of the Catholic Church's mission to non-Christian migrants as, first and foremost, "the witness of Christian charity, which itself has an evangelizing value that may open hearts for the explicit proclamation of the gospel when this is done with due Christian prudence and full respect for the freedom of the other" (59).

In the second instance, FEISA V states that the Asian church "can and should take the initiative of providing pastoral care to migrants with inter-religious dimensions" (Eilers 2007, 129). It explains that the Asian church should not only "see and understand the dignity of other faiths" but also receive and assist these migrants in their moment of greatest need, taking the initiative to reach out and visit them because as non-Catholics, they "may not have the courage to visit Catholic churches" (119). It suggests that local parishes could offer space and hospitality to these migrants who "need a place where they can gather together for prayers or to have their religious celebrations or just for a friendly gathering among themselves" (120; see 130). Here, FEISA V affirms what Pope John Paul II had said in his message for the eighty-eighth World Day of Migration, entitled "Migration and Inter-religious Dialogue": "The parish represents the space in which a true pedagogy of meeting with people of various religious convictions and cultures can be realized. . . . The parish community can become a training ground of hospitality, a place where an exchange of experiences and gifts takes place. This cannot but foster a tranquil life together, preventing the risk of tension with immigrants who bring other religious beliefs with themselves. . . . Every day, in many parts of the world, migrants, refugees and displaced people turn to Catholic organizations and parishes in search of support, and they are welcome irrespective of cultural or religious affiliation" (2002, 3, 5).

Hence FEISA V also emphasizes the need to give special attention to refugees and internally displaced persons as an outgrowth of the church's ministry to the poor, oppressed, and marginalized

(Eilers 2007, 114). Specifically, it insists that the Asian church needs to include ecumenism and interreligious dialogue in its outreach work with refugees because the church "is most critical in this region where we belong to the minority and we work in the midst of rich, diverse, and important religious and cultural traditions. The spirit of ecumenism and interreligious dialogue should thus permeate our programming processes. While our faith spurs us to serve the refugees it does not become the criteria for refugees to avail themselves of our services" (117).

Finally, in recognition of the fact that trained pastoral workers are needed to engage with migrants in the fullness of their cultures, religions, and poverty, FEISA V makes the following recommendation: "To fully understand the needs of the migrants, the Church must equip herself with the knowledge and skills required for this minority. These include knowledge of the languages of migrants, the provision of possibilities for migrants to express their faith with their language and culture, if necessary, of missionaries capable to be with migrants or mediators of faith and cultural dialogue" (Eilers 2007, 130). This point is also echoed by *Erga migrantes caritas Christi*, which suggests that "the ordinary Catholic faithful and pastoral workers in local Churches should receive solid formation and information on other religions so as to overcome prejudices, prevail over religious relativism and avoid unjustified suspicions and fears that hamper dialogue and erect barriers, even provoking violence or misunderstanding" (Pontifical Council for the Pastoral Care of Migrants and Itinerant People 2004, 69). Without a doubt, FEISA V unequivocally repudiates the temptation to proselytize among non-Christian migrants in their most vulnerable state when it calls for pastoral workers to learn the languages, cultures, and traditions of these non-Christian migrants, enabling them to possess the relevant skills and abilities to interact with these migrants and assist them in retaining and expressing their own languages, cultures, and religious faiths.

Transient Migrants

From the foregoing discussion, we see that the FABC has chosen to focus on migrants who make a *permanent* and *unidirectional* move from their homelands to new countries, whether they are economic migrants, who could be documented or undocumented, or refugees or asylum seekers. In the various statements and documents from the FABC that we have examined, it is clear that the FABC's principal spotlight is on the pastoral outreach to as well as the care of permanent migrants in diasporic communities who are usually unable to return to their homelands for a variety of reasons, whether they are internally displaced migrants, migrants who flee their homelands because of persecution or war, or economic migrants who leave for better opportunities abroad. Hence the FABC's theological and pastoral responses have centered on the marginalized status of these migrants who have made a permanent break from their homelands and are now living in various diasporic communities across Asia, seeking to address and resolve the many complex intercultural and interreligious issues that emerge when different ethnic, social, cultural, and religious dimensions of migrants and their hosts are brought together in an explosive mix.

In this section, I will discuss a growing form of migration in Asia that has yet to catch the attention of the FABC—the phenomenon of *transient migrants* as distinct from *permanent migrants*—as well as explore its implications for the FABC and the Asian church. Since the beginning of the twenty-first century, sociologists have begun to pay attention to a new category of migration called *transient migration* as distinct from *permanent migration* and which emerges as the result of transnational forces that shape *ongoing multiple recurrent migrations* rather than a singular, linear, and unidirectional migration. In a seminal essay entitled "From International Migration to Transnational Diaspora," Korean American sociologist John Lie argues that the classic immigration narrative of a "singular, break from the old country to the new nation" is no longer tenable or viable in view of a world that is becoming increasingly global, transnational, and intertwined (1995, 303). Lie argues as follows: "It is no longer assumed that immigrants make a sharp break from their homelands. Rather pre-immigration networks, cultures, and capital remain salient. The sojourn itself is neither unidirectional nor final. Multiple, circular and return migrations, rather than a single great journey from one sedentary space to another, occur across transnational spaces. People's movements, in other words, follow multifarious trajectories and sustain diverse networks" (304). More importantly, Lie suggests that transnational and global forces subvert the "unidirectionality of migrant passage; circles, returns, and multiple movements follow the waxing and waning structures of opportunities and networks" (305).

It is in this context of recurrent transnational migrations that the Asian Australian sociologist Catherine Gomes has coined the terms *transient migration* and *transient mobility* to focus attention on those "transient migrants" who are constantly on the move and not looking to stay in a particular location permanently or for the long term. In two essays that Gomes and I coauthored together, Gomes uses the terms *transient migrants, transient migration,* and *transient mobility* to refer to the global and transnational movements of people for work, study, and lifestyle, including skilled professionals and students in pursuit of international education (Gomes and Tan 2015; Gomes and Tan 2017). In other words, transient migrants are not looking for permanent residency or citizenship in new lands. They are neither fleeing their homelands nor seeking asylum in third countries. Instead, they are taking advantage of their transnational mobility in a globalized economy to use their professional skills to further their careers in a variety of different countries before retiring either in their home countries or elsewhere.

On the one hand, the concept of transient migrants is not new. Indeed, existing theological scholarship has focused attention on *unskilled* transient migrants, especially foreign domestic workers, discussing important theological implications of their plight and articulating pastoral responses to their lack of agency, ill-treatment, and poor working conditions (see Cruz 2010; Parreñas 2001). On the other hand, theologians have paid comparatively scant attention to the growing transient migration and transient mobility of educated skilled professionals and international students. More significantly, a significant proportion of the populations of the oil-rich Persian Gulf States of the Arabian Peninsula and the global financial hubs in Asia such as Singapore and Hong Kong is transient migrants. For example, close to 30 percent of Singapore's population—that is, 1.6 million of the 5.47 million living in Singapore—are transient migrants on various types of employment or student passes who are not entitled to permanent residency or citizenship in Singapore (Gomes and Tan 2015, 219). Increasingly, Christian transient migrants outnumber and overshadow local Christians in Hong Kong, Taiwan, and Japan, judging from the growing number of English, Tagalog, and Bahasa Indonesia services in these places compared to services in local languages such as Cantonese, Mandarin, or Japanese.

More significantly, these educated transient migrants, whether skilled professionals or international students, comprise one of the prime drivers of the growth of Christianity around the world generally and in Asia in particular, as they move across cities, countries, and continents in search of the next professional job assignment or higher education prospects. In this regard, Gomes's fieldwork among transient migrants who are either skilled professionals or university-going international students in Singapore and Melbourne reveals the active role that Christianity plays in the identity constructions and social networking for many of these people. Gomes herself notes that while she and her research assistants did not specifically go out to investigate Christianity among transient migrants, they discover that "the Christian faith featured prominently in the answers of a number of respondents" in Singapore, with more than one-third—that is, thirty out of eighty-eight—of the respondents identifying as Christian (Gomes and Tan 2015, 225). In our analysis of the interviews of these respondents, we arrive at the following conclusion: "The results revealed that Asian foreign talent transient migrants who identified themselves as Christian turn to Christianity as a way of coping with everyday life in transience. On one level, the Christian groups they join allow them to create a sense of community while being away from the home nation. *This sense of community, however, is with other Asian foreign transient migrants, rather than with locals*, such as sharing the same nationality and ethnicity dominate. The results of this study contribute to ongoing intersecting discussions on the (transient) migration experience, community and Christianity" (226; emphasis added). We also observe how Christianity provides a framework for these transient migrants to develop resilience in order to cope with the various challenges of transience that they experience in their lives: "Respondents [in Singapore] noted that they actively struck up friendships with people in order to help cope with the traumas of their voluntary uprootedness, with Christianity being a key feature in this quest. Of the thirty participants interviewed, a quarter of them alleviated these conditions by making friends with people from their respective churches. While a few participants were already Christian before coming to Singapore such as the Filipino Catholics and Indonesian Christians, others found Christianity while living in the island-state" (228).

It is not surprising that the majority of transient migrants, whether Christians or converts to Christianity, choose to join congregations with fellow transient migrants rather than with local Singaporeans, experiencing a "community in transience" with fellow Christian transient migrants (Gomes and Tan 2015,

227). In other words, for many, if not the majority of the transient migrants in Singapore who embrace Christianity and make it a part of their identity constructions as transient migrants, their Christian faith becomes an important and defining aspect of who they are, affording them an opportunity to maintain their own Christian identity apart from Singaporean Christians. Gomes's ethnographic study of international students in Melbourne, Australia, also reveals similar developments: "Melbourne . . . is home to several significant churches catering to international students, including the Cross Culture Church. Situated in the heart of the city, the Cross Culture Church, which belongs to the Churches of Christ denomination, has services in English and Mandarin and one of its pastors is dedicated to ministering specifically to international students. . . . Even the serviced apartment complex Arrow on Swanston, which almost exclusively caters to international students during semester sessions, has church facilities in its basement and likewise holds regular Sunday services" (Gomes and Tan 2017, 188).

Hence our findings highlight the implications of transient migration and transient migrants for Asian Christianity generally and the complex relationships between transient migrants and the local Christian communities in particular. Because these transient migrants are not looking to immigrate permanently, hence the term *transient*, their sense of Christian belonging and identity is not with the local Christian communities but rather with their fellow Christians who are transient migrants like themselves, as our fieldwork has shown. In turn, this challenges how local Christian communities relate to and engage with their Christian sisters and brothers who are transient migrants. While Gomes's fieldwork focuses on Evangelical Christian transient migrants in Singapore and Melbourne, one should not think that this is merely an Evangelical Christian phenomenon. Asian Catholics also comprise a growing percentage of transient migrants, especially in Hong Kong and Japan, where Catholic transient migrants are increasing in number compared to local Catholics. More importantly, the challenges of Asian Catholic transient migrants come to the forefront in the Persian Gulf States of the Arabian Peninsula, which we will examine in greater detail below.

Asian Catholic Transient Migrants in the Persian Gulf States

The oil-rich Persian Gulf States of the Arabian Peninsula, encompassing the six wealthy nation-states of Bahrain, Kuwait, Oman, Qatar, Saudi Arabia, and the United Arab Emirates (UAE), have all witnessed a rapid growth in transient migrant professionals in the petroleum, engineering, construction, medical, and hospitality sectors, contributing to the rapid growth of Christianity in the Arabian Peninsula, which has long been dominated by Islam. In his March 8, 2014, article in the *Boston Globe*, columnist John L. Allen Jr. notes that the Arabian Peninsula is witnessing dramatic Catholic growth rates that are driven not by Arab converts but by Asian Catholic transient migrants with no rights to permanent residency or citizenship: "The result is a Catholic population on the peninsula estimated at around 2.5 million. Kuwait and Qatar are home to between 350,000 and 400,000 Catholics, Bahrain has about 140,000 and Saudi Arabia itself has 1.5 million" (Allen 2014). The bulk of these Catholic transient migrants are Filipino Catholics (Brazal and Odchigue 2016), with Indian Catholics comprising the second largest cohort, followed by Pakistanis, Bangladeshis, Sri Lankans, Lebanese, Palestinians, Iraqis, and Southeast Asians.

Juridically, the Arabian Peninsula is divided into two apostolic vicariates:[1] the Apostolic Vicariate of Northern Arabia (www.avona.org), which comprises the Gulf States of Bahrain, Kuwait, Qatar, and Saudi Arabia, with the official seat in Bahrain, and the Apostolic Vicariate of Southern Arabia (www.avosa.org), covering the Gulf States of Oman, UAE, and Yemen, with the official seat in Abu

Dhabi, UAE. The oldest Catholic church in the Arabian Peninsula is the historic Sacred Heart Church (www.sacredheartchurchbahrain .org) in Manama, the capital of Bahrain, which was dedicated on Christmas Eve 1939. On February 11, 2013, King Hamad bin Isa Al Khalifa of Bahrain donated nine thousand square meters of land in Awali, about 20 km south of Manama, for the construction of a new cathedral to be dedicated to Our Lady of Arabia (www .bahraincathedral.org) as the official seat for the Apostolic Vicariate of Northern Arabia with an anticipated completion date of the end of 2021. The largest Catholic parish church worldwide is not in Europe or North America but rather in Dubai, UAE, in the Apostolic Vicariate of Southern Arabia—Saint Mary's Catholic Church in Dubai (www.saintmarysdubai.org), which has over three hundred thousand parishioners, all of whom are Catholic transient migrants working in Dubai, with thirty-five to forty weekend Masses in twelve languages and over eighty thousand hosts distributed weekly. In 2014, the nightly Simbang Gabi Masses—that is, a novena of nine Masses leading up to Christmas at Saint Mary's in Dubai—drew crowds of more than fifteen thousand Filipino Catholics each night, resulting in the Simbang Gabi Masses being celebrated in the church's parking lot to accommodate everyone.[2]

Unlike Dubai and Bahrain, Saudi Arabia—with the largest concentration of Catholic transient migrants, many of whom are Filipino Catholics—has refused to grant permission for the building of churches, whether Catholic or Protestant. In this ecclesial vacuum, the Catholic Charismatic Renewal Movement (CCRM) generally and the Gulf Catholic Charismatic Renewal Services (GCCRS) in particular, as well as individual Catholic charismatic groups such as the Filipino El Shaddai Catholic charismatic movement, play a very important role for the maintenance and nourishment of the faith life of these Catholic transient migrants.[3] In this challenging situation, charismatic prayer groups not only empower lay Catholic transient migrants as prophets, exorcists, healers, and lay leaders but also enable them to transcend political borders and circumvent legal restrictions on churches and clergy presence. This has enabled lay Catholic transient migrants to assume leadership and responsibility for keeping the Christian faith alive and strong among their fellow Catholic transient migrants in Saudi Arabia and elsewhere across the Persian Gulf States of the Arabian Peninsula.

Not surprisingly, the Catholic charismatic movement's empowerment of lay leadership and participation has kindled the fire that has led to its explosive growth across the globe generally and in Asia in particular. In Asia, the charismatic movement has swept through much of Asia, transforming Asian Christianity in general and Asian Catholics in particular. Asia joins Africa and Latin America in having a sizeable number of Pentecostal and charismatic Christians. The CCRM took root in Asia in the late 1960s in the aftermath of Vatican II (1962–65). Since the charismatic movement caught fire among Asian Catholics in the 1970s, the CCRM has experienced tremendous growth throughout Asia. According to the latest statistics compiled by the Vatican-backed International Catholic Charismatic Renewal Services (ICCRS), there are nearly fourteen thousand charismatic prayer groups in the Asian church, with an estimated 15 percent of Asian Catholics involved in the CCRM. Indeed, Asia comes second after Latin America, which has an estimated 16 percent of Catholics involved in the CCRM (John 2010).[4]

The CCRM in Asia received a big boost in 1994 with the formation of the Catholic Charismatic Council for Asia-Pacific under the aegis of the ICCRS. As a result of the efforts of various local leaders in building and promoting the CCRM within various regions of Asia, the tremendous growth of the CCRM throughout Asia caught the attention of the ICCRS, which established the ICCRS Subcommittee for Asia-Oceania (ISAO) in December 2006 at a meeting in Singapore that drew participants from fourteen countries in the Asia-Oceania region. The ISAO organized the first Asia-Oceania

Catholic Charismatic Renewal Leaders' Conference in Jakarta, Indonesia, from September 14 to 18, 2008, which drew 525 CCRM leaders from twenty-one countries in the Asia-Oceania region, marking an important milestone in the awakening of the Spirit in the revival of the Asian Catholic Church. This was followed by the establishment of the GCCRS, which held its inaugural conference from December 7 to 9, 2008, which drew 1,800 leaders from Bahrain, Kuwait, Oman, Qatar, Saudi Arabia, and the UAE under the banner "Let the Fire Fall Again." The sizeable number of leaders from these six Persian Gulf States of the Arabian Peninsula is testimony to the power and influence of lay Catholic charismatic leaders in organizing and nourishing the faith of their fellow Catholic transient migrants in the absence of churches and clergy to maintain the traditional Catholic sacramental life. This 2008 conference paved the way for Asia to have the honor of hosting in South Korea from June 2 to 9, 2009, the International Catholic Charismatic Leaders' Conference. This was the first time that this global conference was held outside of Italy. Drawing participants from forty-three countries around the world, this conference culminated in a charismatic prayer rally that drew around fifty thousand participants. This was an important milestone and coming-of-age for the CCRM in Asia, enabling Asia to take its place alongside Latin America and Africa as regions where the CCRM is growing and thriving.

Transient Migrants and Online Communities: A New Way of Being Church

In response to the tight restrictions on churches and clergy, Catholic transient migrants in the Persian Gulf States of the Arabian Peninsula are also breaking boundaries when they create online communities and form virtual "cyberchurches" to circumvent legal restrictions on churches and clergy. Digital presence and online communities that are shaped by social media and mediated by livestreaming and messaging apps are redefining the traditional boundaries of church and Christianity, paving the way for a global and transnational Christianity that is also being realized in virtual presence and online communities. Agnes M. Brazal and Randy Odchigue's essay entitled "Cyberchurch and Filipin@ Migrants in the Middle East" is an important preliminary ethnographic study on how Filipino Catholic transient migrants are creating online faith communities and utilizing Facebook, YouTube videos, livestreaming of Sunday Eucharist and other liturgies, email lists and discussion groups, and other online resources to stay in touch with other Filipino Catholic transient migrants and practice their Christian faith in the absence of churches and clergy (2016, 190–91). For their essay, Brazal and Odchigue interviewed eight Filipino Catholic transient migrants—four in Saudi Arabia who are a graphic artist, caregiver, mechanic, and engineer and four in the UAE who are an electrical engineer, company administrator, teacher, and machine operator, respectively (187–88). What is noteworthy here is how these Filipino Catholic transient migrants in the Persian Gulf States maintain their Catholic identity and nourish their faith using social media and other online tools to create online communities of faith that transcend geographical borders and get around political restrictions on churches operating in those states. This paradigm shift toward online or virtual communities of faith is redefining what it means to be Christian, as well as demonstrating a new way of being church that breaks the traditional geographical parochial boundaries and clerical leadership of such churches.

This major paradigm shift by transient migrants toward online communities that define and nourish their transient migrant and Christian faith identities is not limited to Filipino Catholic transient migrants in the Persian Gulf States of the Arabian Peninsula. We see the same developments in the transient migrants in Singapore and Melbourne who Catherine Gomes surveyed. For example, an

Indonesian information technology person in Singapore speaks of nourishing his Christian faith through online downloads and Christian YouTube channels featuring pastors and preachers (Gomes and Tan 2015, 226). Other examples illustrate how the transient Christian identity is often nourished and maintained by social media platforms such as Facebook and Instagram and messaging apps such as Weibo, QQ, Renren, and WeChat, all of which are popular with transient migrants from mainland China, as well as WhatsApp and LINE for transient migrants from other parts of Asia (Gomes and Tan 2017, 190).

Insider Movements: A New Way of Following Jesus in Asia

The term *insider movements* was first introduced by Scott Moreau in his book *Contextualization in World Missions: Mapping and Assessing Evangelical Models*. Moreau identifies "insider movements" as "movements to obedient faith in Christ that remain integrated with or *inside* their natural community" (2012, 161). Although Moreau is responsible for the term *insider movement*, he is not the first to study this movement. In his groundbreaking book *Churchless Christianity*, Herbert E. Hoefer analyzed the phenomenon of communities of believers in Jesus Christ who chose not to identify with or join Christianity or Christian churches, referring to these believers as "nonbaptized believers in Christ," concluding that it was possible to be a believer in Jesus without identifying as Christian and joining a Christian church (2001; see also Talman and Travis 2015).

Although insider movements are often misunderstood at best, and criticized as heretical at worst by mainstream Christian theologians and clergy, they nevertheless represent a significant development of emergent communities of faith that, by virtue of their theological hybridity and ecclesial-communal double belonging, present profound implications for rethinking theology generally and ecclesiology and missiology in particular (Dyrness 2016; Duerksen and Dyrness 2019). Examples of emergent Muslim followers in Jesus across the Islamic world include Chrislam in Nigeria (Janson 2016; Williams 2019) and the Magindanon followers of Isa al-Masih (Jesus, the Messiah / Christ) in Mindanao, Philippines (Acoba 2013; Yango 2016; see Greenlee 2013). Examples of Buddhist followers of Jesus include the New Buddhists in Thailand, who follow Jesus while retaining a dual belonging to their Buddhist tradition (Tan 2014; Wetchgama 2014). Examples of emergent insider movements of Hindu followers of Jesus in India include the Evangelical-centric Yeshu Satsangs (Duerksen 2015; Hoefer 2002) and the charismatic Catholic Khrist Bhakta movements, which we will discuss below.

Insider movements are especially relevant to the question of Asian Christianity. While the per capita percentage of the population of Christians in Asia has remained stable despite ongoing intense missionary activity, the numbers of Christians increase once we factor in those followers of Jesus in Asia who, nonetheless, eschew baptism and ecclesial membership in favor of remaining within their own cultural and religious communities across Asia. While space does not permit an extensive study of different insider movements in Asia, the example of the Khrist Bhakta movement is redefining what it means to be a follower of Jesus outside of traditional Eurocentric ecclesial structures and membership norms.

Khrist Bhakta Movement

In India, an emerging charismatic movement with profound ecclesiological and liturgical implications is the Khrist Bhakta movement.[5] The Khrist Bhaktas are Indian devotees of Yesubhagavan (Christ

Jesus) as their Satguru—that is, the true Lord and teacher who shall lead them along the path of new life and spiritual growth. They draw spiritual nourishment from Christian ashrams, maintaining a dual belonging or hybridized identity as followers of Christ and his gospel while not formally seeking baptism and Church membership in order to retain their Hindu identities (Sylvester 2013a, 345). Although the Khrist Bhaktas are not, strictly speaking, Catholics, as they neither seek baptism nor participate in the traditional Catholic sacramental life, they nonetheless demonstrate the future direction of hybridized or dual/multiple-belonging Indian Catholic charismatic faith and practice that confounds the institutional structures and boundaries of classical forms of Christian identity and church membership that first emerged in late antique Europe.

The Khrist Bhakta movement is the vision and brainchild of Fr. Anil Dev, an Indian Catholic priest and missioner of the Indian Missionary Society (IMS) who started the movement in 1993 at Matridham Ashram. Founded and operated by the IMS in the midst of the Hindu heartland of Varanasi, Matridham Ashram represents a unique Indian Catholic experiment that seeks to provide a liminal space for hybridized Hindu bhakti (devotional) and Indian Catholic charismatic expressions of spiritual formation and faith development. IMS missioner Jerome Sylvester undertook an ethnographical study of the Khrist Bhakta movement between 2003 and 2007. The survey reveals that the Scheduled Castes make up about 37.3 percent of the Khrist Bhaktas. Sylvester further notes that the majority of Khrist Bhaktas are from the subaltern Scheduled Castes and tribal communities across northern India (2013a, 348). While Matridham Ashram remains the spiritual heartland of the Khrist Bhakta movement, newer communities have emerged across northern India, including Jeevan Dham (Faridabad, near New Delhi), Yesu Darbar (Allahabad), Jabalpur (Madhya Pradesh), Uttar Pradesh, Ranchi (Jharkhand), Patna (Bihar), and Haryana (345–48).

Eschewing the path of baptism for membership in the Indian Catholic Church, most Khrist Bhaktas opt to maintain a hybridized identity, remaining in the *liminal* space of the interstices between Hinduism and charismatic Christianity and participating in weekly charismatic prayer meetings with laying of hands and healings called *satsangs* that combine aspects of rituals of liturgical tradition with devotionals (bhakti), feasting (*melâ*), healing, and exorcisms that are led by lay leaders called *aguwas* (Sylvester 2013b, 448, 452, 453). The *satsangs* are well attended, and numbers grow as a result of testimonies of miracles and healings from the participants.

From his fieldwork among the Khrist Bhaktas, Jerome Sylvester notes that the Khrist Bhaktas seek to combine traditional Indian devotional practices with devotional and ritual elements from the charismatic movement (2013b, 450). Sylvester unpacks the implications of the Khrist Bhakta movement as follows: "The Khristbhaktas are trying to create a social space for themselves in different ways by affirming their experience in Christ. They have found the Khristbhakta Movement as one of the channels. Emancipation and empowerment become the driving force that draws them to the Movement. They find support and shelter in features of free association in the Satsang. The movement is free in every sense of the word, no membership and no limiting structures" (448).

A New Way of Being Church and Following Jesus

On the one hand, the FABC has not engaged directly with Asian Christian transient migrants and their experiences of online and virtual communities, as well as the growing insider movements across Asia that are impacting the shape and direction of Asian Christianity. On the other hand, the time has come for the FABC to consider seriously the profound implications of these communities for reshaping its ecclesiology and missiology in the context of shifting ecclesial landscapes within a rapidly changing contemporary postcolonial Asia that is buffeted by the forces of globalization and transnationalism. When the FABC pays attention to the daily lived experiences of Christians across Asia, how does it map the social and virtual geographies of the changing faces of Asian Christianity beyond the shapes, structures, and boundaries that have been established by Eurocentric ecclesiologies? Within the framework of its regnocentric theology of the Reign of God in Asia, how would the FABC reenvision the contours of its ecclesiology to take into account the theological implications of Asian transient migrants, transient migrants creating and participating in online and virtual faith communities, and the challenges and opportunities posed by the growing insider movements across Asia?

In the past, the grounded geography of Christianity meant that the institutional church is structured on communities of faith meeting in physical buildings that are built in specific geographical regions. Ecclesiologies and theologies have been constructed, debated, and shaped by the needs and aspirations of faith communities who gather for worship, fellowship, and communal life in those buildings in specific geographical locations. This is true even for the FABC's new way of being church and doing Christian mission in postcolonial Asia, including its missional engagements with the peoples who are on the move across Asia. The growth of Asian Christian transient migrant communities poses new challenges and opportunities for the FABC. As we have seen in this chapter, many transient migrants often turn to Christianity as well as virtual and online communities of faith in their quest for finding meaning, networking, and constructing their own faith and social identities. One could certainly argue that virtual and online communities nourish the *resilience* of these transient migrants in the face of the many challenges of living in transience.

On the one hand, the 1.5 million Catholics in Saudi Arabia cannot legally build a church or gather for a Sunday Eucharist that is presided by an ordained priest. On the other hand, Asian Catholic transient migrants in Saudi Arabia can turn to social media, livestreaming, and online communities to create virtual or online church beyond the reach of Saudi law. Indeed, without social media and online communities, there is no church in Saudi Arabia. Hence social media and online communities are redefining the boundaries of what it means to be church in Asia, reimagining church and pastoral ministry, shaping a virtual ecclesiology, and posing new questions for theology on the issues of faith and identity formation in transience.

More importantly, while transience may be *lo cotidiano* for transient migrants, it is still an experience in uprootedness, loneliness, and a yearning for home. Historically, as a universal religion that spread throughout the world because of transnational movements, Christianity plays an important role in helping transient migrants make sense of themselves and their faith experiences in strange and unfamiliar settings (Gomes and Tan 2015, 233–34). Yet just because transient migrants embrace Christianity and make Christianity a part of their identity, it does not necessarily signal their assimilation into the broader host society or acceptance by their fellow Christians in their host society. Taking Christian transient migrants in Singapore as an example, by embracing Christianity on their own terms, these transient migrants "have consciously forced religious identities in opposition to the discrimination they have encountered" despite their shared Christian faith with Singaporean Christians because they have "created institutions that reflect their concerns and cater to their own needs" (234).

In other words, the transnational Christianity of transient migrants can and does exist alongside indigenous or local Christianity because of the differing worldviews and expectations of these transient migrants and the locals who are citizens and permanent residents. This would have profound implications for the FABC to consider in terms of ecclesiology and catholicity, especially the tensions between a universal vision of faith and church vis-à-vis the particularity of diversity and pluralism as well as the xenophobia of local Christians toward their transient migrant counterparts notwithstanding a shared Christian faith. Indeed, Catherine Gomes and I see this in the majority of the Christian transient migrants in Singapore, as we conclude,

> For many, if not the majority of these Asian foreign talent transient migrants who embrace their Christian faith and make it a part of their diasporic identity in Singapore, their Christian identity becomes an important and defining aspect of who they are, enabling them to communicate with Singaporean Christians, yet affording them the opportunity to carve out a niche where they can define their own identity apart from their fellow Singaporean Christians . . . leading to heterogenized, hybridized, and conflicting constructions of faith identity that simultaneously connect yet distance themselves from other Singaporean Christians. It is important to note that when Asian foreign talent transient migrants embrace a Christian faith identity, often with more fervour than they do in their homelands, this goes beyond mere nostalgic longing for home to encompass new opportunities for them to shape their own transnational, hybridized, and often contested multiplicity of identities in Singapore, where they are at best tolerated or at worse vilified by Singaporeans who express varying degrees of xenophobia against them. (Gomes and Tan 2015, 234–35)

Likewise, insider movements are changing the face of Asian Christianity, as their adherents cross multiple boundaries, engage in complex multiple belongings, and construct new convergences of hybridized personal identities and multifaceted communal faith identities that challenge the traditional ecclesial boundaries of classical forms of Christian identity and church membership. While the per capita percentage of the population of Christians in Asia has remained stable despite ongoing intense missionary activity, the numbers increase once we factor in those followers of Jesus who, nonetheless, eschew baptism and ecclesial membership in favor of remaining within their own cultural and religious communities across Asia.

More importantly, insider movements as emergent movements within postcolonial Asian Christianity reveal the complexities of multiple belongings and hybridized identities that challenge the homogeneity of the ecclesiological vision of Eurocentric Christianity. By putting at the center of their faith life their hybridized devotional and popular ritual practices rather than Eurocentric church structures, membership, and worship practices, these subaltern Asians are challenging the hegemony of a Eurocentric institutional vision of church.

In contrast to the experiences of transient migrants who are educated professionals or international students, insider movements hail primarily from the subaltern classes of people across the majority world who are confronting the challenges of postcolonialism, postmodernism, and globalization that are rapidly transforming the world around them. Although Jerome Sylvester made these remarks in the context of Khrist Bhaktas, they are pertinent to the marginal status of other subaltern groups in other insider movements that reject official ecclesial identities for hybridized identities: "The subaltern struggle against caste and class can be well understood against the background of heterodox and antisystemic movements. Those who are at the margins negotiate the porous borders in their search of a new identity and empowerment. Khristbhaktas negotiate the borders of faith and culture for empowerment against social exclusion and marginalization from the liminal position of Hinduism and Christianity" (2013a, 348–49). In the final analysis, although transient migrants and insider movements appear to be living in separate worlds, they do share much in common in the sense that they live hybridized lives where they do not often fit neatly into the mainstream society around them. Faith in Jesus Christ becomes a *means of resilience* in the face of the challenges of everyday life "betwixt and between" in transience as transient migrants, online communities, and insider movements transgress the borders and redefine the boundaries of emergent Asian Christianity for the future ahead, setting out a new way of being church and following Jesus in postcolonial Asia.

Notes

Chapter 2

1 For critical evaluations of the Federation of Asian Bishops' Conferences' (FABC's) history, impact, and achievements, see Arévalo 1992; Wilfred 1992; Fox 2002; and Chia 2003.

Chapter 4

1 See also *Asian Colloquium on Ministries in the Church*, 25, 26, and 27 (in Rosales and Arévalo 1992, 72–73); and FABC III, 3.1, 3.2, and 8.1 (in Rosales and Arévalo 1992, 54, 56–57).

Chapter 5

1 The term "church *sui iuris*" (*ecclesia sui iuris*) defines a church under a hierarchy of bishops that is properly constituted in accordance with ecclesiocanonical norms and recognized as autonomous by the supreme authority of the universal church. In the Code of Canons of the Eastern Churches (*Codex Canonum Ecclesiarum Orientalium*, or CCEO), "church *sui iuris*" refers to a distinct church with its own ecclesial heritage and self-government (see Vatican 1990, canons 27

and 174). In the past, the churches *sui iuris* were erroneously called "rites"—for example, the Latin-Rite Church, Byzantine-Rite Church, and so on. This erroneous usage was based on a now abandoned ecclesiological paradigm of absorbing those Eastern churches that had sought communion with the See of Peter into union within the "single" universal church with its seat in Rome but allowing them to maintain their canonical disciplines and liturgical traditions as "rites." With the promulgation of the CCEO in 1990, the usage of terms such as *rites* and *uniate churches* are no longer tenable. Properly speaking, the term *rite* refers to a *whole tradition* of an ecclesial community, which includes its liturgical, theological, spiritual, sociocultural, and disciplinary heritages. Therefore, a church *sui iuris* is a juridically distinct church within the broader framework of a "rite," or tradition. Strictly speaking, there are six rites—Latin, Alexandrian (Coptic), Antiochene, Armenian, Chaldean, and Byzantine—but there are twenty-three Eastern Catholic churches *sui iuris* in communion with the Latin Church under the See of Peter, making a total of twenty-four Catholic churches within the Catholic communion.

2 For the history, ecclesial identity, and liturgical practices of these patriarchal churches, see Roberson 2008.

3 For a history of the Syro-Malabar Church, the Syro-Malankara Church, and the Saint Thomas Christians, see Roberson 2008.

4 Notwithstanding its name, the Catholic Bishops' Conference of India (CBCI) is, strictly speaking, not an "episcopal conference" as defined by canon 447 of the Code of Canon Law 1983, which in the Indian context is the Latin Catholic Church's Conference of Catholic Bishops of India (CCBI). Rather, as an umbrella organization, the CBCI is similar to the Federation of Asian Bishops' Conferences (FABC) in the sense that it is a "federation" or "permanent association of Catholic Bishops of India" for the whole of India, comprising the Eastern Catholic and Latin Catholic *sui iuris* churches as full members. The CBCI was formally constituted in September 1944 at the Conference of Metropolitans in Chennai (Madras), India, with the principal objectives of coordinating between the three *sui iuris* Indian Catholic churches (Syro-Malabar, Syro-Malankara, and Latin Catholic [CBCI]) on shared issues and questions as well as working on common policy making, external representation, and advocacy on behalf of all three member churches with various political, governmental, religious, and social bodies in India.

Chapter 6

1 An *apostolic vicariate* refers to a mission territory where a diocese
has not yet been canonically named and erected, which is under the
direct jurisdiction of the Roman pontiff as the vicar of the church
universal, who exercises his jurisdiction through the appointment of an
apostolic vicar as his representative instead of a local bishop. As mission
territories, apostolic vicariates come under the supervision of the
Congregation for the Evangelization of Peoples (formerly known as
the Congregation for the Propagation of the Faith, or Propaganda Fide).

2 The information and statistics on Saint Mary's Catholic Church in
Dubai come from my personal communication with Filipino American
theologian Ricky Manalo, who visited Saint Mary's in December 2014
and observed the weekend Masses and nightly Simbang Gabi Masses.

3 Established in 1981 by Mike Velarde, El Shaddai has spread like wildfire
among Filipino Catholics in the Philippines as well as in the global
Filipino diaspora, garnering a following of about eleven million within
fifteen years, with chapters in nearly every province in the Philippines
and more than thirty-five countries around the world. For an in-depth
examination of El Shaddai, as well as its growth and impact on Filipino
Catholicism, see Wiegele 2005.

4 Cyril John (2010), the vice president of ICCRS, presented his
unpublished paper titled "Lay Movements and New Communities
in the Life and Mission of the Church in Asia: Experiences from the
Catholic Charismatic Renewal" at the Congress of Asian Catholic Laity,
which met from August 31 to September 5, 2010, in Seoul, South Korea.

5 For in-depth ethnographical and theological discussions of the Khrist
Bhakta movement, see Sylvester 2013a, 2013b, 2013c; Kuttiyanikkal
2014; and San Chirico 2014.

References

Legislation Cited

Malaysia Federal Constitution, August 31, 1957, revised November 1, 2010.

Case Law Cited

Lina Joy v. Majlis Agama Islam Wilayah Persekutuan dan lain-lain, (2007) 4
MLJ 585 (Federal Court, Malaysia).
*Menteri Dalam Negeri & Ors v. Titular Roman Catholic Archbishop of Kuala
Lumpur,* (2013) 6 MLJ 468 (Court of Appeal, Malaysia).
*Titular Roman Catholic Archbishop of Kuala Lumpur v. Menteri Dalam
Negeri and Kerajaan Malaysia,* (2010) 2 MLJ 78 (High Court, Malaysia).
*Titular Roman Catholic Archbishop of Kuala Lumpur v. Menteri Dalam Negeri
and Others,* (2014) 4 MLJ 765 (Federal Court, Malaysia).

Books and Articles Cited

Abbott, Walter M., ed. 1966. *The Documents of Vatican II: All Sixteen Official
Texts Promulgated by the Ecumenical Council 1963–1965 Translated from
the Latin.* New York: America Press.

⬛

Acoba, E. [pseud.]. 2013. "Towards an Understanding of Inclusivity in Contextualizing into Philippine Context." In *The Gospel in Culture: Contextualization Issues through Asian Eyes*, edited by Melba Padilla Maggay, 416–450. Manila: OMF Literature.

Agrawal, D. P. 1982. *The Archaeology of India*. London: Curzon.

Aikman, David. 2003. *Jesus in Beijing: How Christianity Is Transforming China and Changing the Global Balance of Power*. Washington, DC: Regnery.

Allen, John L., Jr. 2014. "Catholicism Growing in Heart of Muslim World." *Boston Globe*, March 8, 2014. tinyurl.com/vptspful.

Amaladoss, Michael. 1988. "Foreign Missions Today." *East Asian Pastoral Review* 25:104–118.

———. 1991. "The Challenges of Mission Today." In *Trends in Mission: Toward the Third Millennium*, edited by William Jenkinson and Helene O'Sullivan, 359–397. Maryknoll, NY: Orbis.

———. 2000. "The Image of Jesus in *The Church in Asia*." *East Asian Pastoral Review* 37:233–241.

———. 2014. "Asian Theological Trends." In *The Oxford Handbook of Christianity in Asia*, edited by Felix Wilfred, 104–120. Oxford: Oxford University Press.

Arévalo, C. G. 1992. "The Time of Heirs." In *For All the Peoples of Asia: Federation of Asian Bishops' Conferences Documents from 1970–1991*, edited by Gaudencio B. Rosales and C. G. Arévalo, xv–xxii. Maryknoll, NY: Orbis.

Ariyaratne, A. T. 1999. "Sarvodaya Shramadana's Approach to Peacebuilding." In *Buddhist Peacework: Creating Cultures of Peace*, edited by David W. Chappell, 69–80. Somerville, MA: Wisdom.

Ashiwa, Yoshiko, and David L. Wank. 2009. *Making Religion, Making the State: The Politics of Religion in Modern China*. Stanford, CA: Stanford University Press.

Bali, Gali. 1998. "Asian Synod and Concerns of the Local Church." *Jeevadhara* 28:297–330.

Bartholomeusz, Tessa J. 2002. *In Defense of Dharma: Just-War Ideology in Buddhist Sri Lanka*. London: Routledge.

Battistella, Graziano. 1995. "For a More Abundant Life: Migrant Workers in Asia." In *Sixth Plenary Assembly Background Paper: Journeying Together in Faith with Migrant Workers in Asia*. FABC paper no. 73, 1–16. Hong Kong: FABC.

Baum, Wilheim Baum, and Dietmar W. Winkler. 2003. *The Church of the East: A Concise History*. London: Routledge Curzon.

Benedict XVI, Pope. 2006. "Address of May 15, 2006 to the Plenary Assembly of the Pontifical Council for Migrants and Travelers." *L'Osservatore Romano*, May 24, 2006.

Bevans, Stephen. 1996. "Inculturation of Theology in Asia (the Federation of Asian Bishops' Conferences, 1970–1995)." *Studia Missionalia* 45:1–23.

Bhatt, Chetan. 2001. *Hindu Nationalism: Origins, Ideologies, and Modern Myths*. New York: Berg.

Blalock, Hubert M. 1967. *Toward a Theory of Minority-Group Relations*. New York: Wiley.

Bonacich, Edna. 1973. "A Theory of Middleman Minorities." *American Sociological Review* 38:583–594.

Boodoo, Gerald M. 2010. "Catholicity and Mission." *Proceedings of the Catholic Theological Society of America* 65:117–118.

Boxer, Charles R. 1969. *The Portuguese Seaborne Empire: 1415–1825*. New York: Knopf.

Brazal, Agnes M., and Randy Odchigue. 2016. "Cyberchurch and Filipin@ Migrants in the Middle East." In *Church in an Age of Global Migration: A Moving Body*, edited by Susanna Snyder, Joshua Ralston, and Agnes M. Brazal, 187–200. New York: Palgrave Macmillan.

Camilleri, Rita. 2013. "Religious Pluralism in Malaysia: The Journey of Three Prime Ministers." *Islam and Christian-Muslim Relations* 24 (2): 225–240.

Catholic Bishops' Conference of India (CBCI). 1998. "Responses to the Lineamenta." *East Asian Pastoral Review* 35:112–129.

———. 2008. "Violence against Christians: Statement of the Executive Body of the Catholic Bishops' Conference of India." *Vidyajyoti Journal of Theological Reflection* 72:814–817.

Chandler, Stuart. 2004. *Establishing a Pure Land on Earth: The Foguang Buddhist Perspective on Modernization and Globalization*. Honolulu: University of Hawai'i Press.

Chang, Kwang-chih. 1986. *The Archaeology of Ancient China*. 4th ed. New Haven, CT: Yale University Press.

Chia, Edmund. 2003. *Thirty Years of FABC: History, Foundation, Context and Theology*. FABC paper no. 106. Hong Kong: FABC.

Chin, James. 2009. "The Malaysian Chinese Dilemma: The Never Ending Policy (NEP)." *Chinese Southern Diaspora Studies* 3:167–182.

Claver, Francisco. 1998. "Personal Thoughts on the Asian Synod." *East Asian Pastoral Review* 35:241–248.

Colombo, Domenico, ed. 1997. *Enchiridion Documenti della Chiesa in Asia: Federazione delle Conferenze Episcopali Asiatiche, 1970–1995*. Bologna: Editrice Missionaria Italiana.

Comber, Leon. 1983. *13 May 1969: A Historical Survey of Sino-Malay Relations*. Kuala Lumpur, Malaysia: Heinemann Asia.

Costa, Horacio de la, and John Schumacher. 1976. *Church and State: The Philippine Experience*. Quezon City, Philippines: Loyola School of Theology.

Crenshaw, Kimberlé. 1989. "Demarginalizing the Intersection of Race and Sex: A Black Feminist Critique of Antidiscrimination Doctrine, Feminist Theory and Antiracist Politics." *University of Chicago Legal Forum* 1989:139–167. https://tinyurl.com/ux4xafbt.

Cruz, Gemma Tulud. 2010. *An Intercultural Theology of Migration: Pilgrims in the Wilderness*. Leiden: Brill.

Darmaatmadja, Cardinal Julius. 1999. "A New Way of Being Church in Asia." Response to Pope John Paul II's address at Delhi cathedral. *Vidyajyoti* 63:887–891.

Deegalle, Mahinda, ed. 2006. *Buddhism, Conflict and Violence in Modern Sri Lanka*. New York: Routledge.

Dinkel, Jürgen. 2019. *The Non-aligned Movement: Genesis, Organization and Politics (1927–1992)*. Leiden: Brill.

Duerksen, Darren T. 2015. *Ecclesial Identities in a Multifaith Context: Jesus Truth-Gatherings (Yeshu-Satsangs) among Hindus and Sikhs in Northwest India*. Eugene, OR: Pickwick.

Duerksen, Darren T., and William A. Dyrness. 2019. *Seeking Church: Emerging Witnesses to the Kingdom*. Downers Grove, IL: IVP Academic.

Dyrness, William A. 2016. *Insider Jesus: Theological Reflections on New Christian Movements*. Downers Grove, IL: IVP Academic.

Eilers, Franz-Josef. 1997. *For All the Peoples of Asia*. Vol. 2, *Federation of Asian Bishops' Conferences Documents from 1992 to 1996*. Quezon City, Philippines: Claretian.

———. 2002. *For All the Peoples of Asia*. Vol. 3, *Federation of Asian Bishops' Conferences Documents from 1997–2001*. Quezon City, Philippines: Claretian.

———. 2007. *For All the Peoples of Asia*. Vol. 4, *Federation of Asian Bishops' Conferences Documents from 2002–2006*. Quezon City, Philippines: Claretian.

Esteves, Sarto. 2005. "Violence against the Cross." In *Religion, Power and Violence: Expression of Politics in Contemporary Times*, edited by Ram Puniyani, 277–289. Thousand Oaks, CA: Sage.

FABC Office of Theological Concerns (formerly Theological Advisory Commission). 1987. *Theses on Interreligious Dialogue: An Essay in Pastoral Theological Reflection.* FABC paper no. 48. Hong Kong: FABC.

———. 1991. *Theses on the Local Church: A Theological Reflection in the Asian Context.* FABC paper no. 60. Hong Kong: FABC.

Federation of Asian Bishops' Conferences (FABC). n.d. "About Us." FABC. Accessed February 17, 2021. http://www.fabc.org/about.html.

Fernandes, Angelo. 1991. "Dialogue in the Context of Asian Realities." *Vidyajyoti Journal of Theological Reflection* 55:545–560.

Fernando, Lorenzo. 2000. "CBCI and FABC on Religious Pluralism." *Vidyajyoti Journal of Theological Reflection* 64:857–869.

Fox, Thomas C. 1998a. "Asian Bishops Remain Politely Persistent." *National Catholic Reporter*, May 8, 1998.

———. 1998b. "Asia Synod Opens with Call for Change." *National Catholic Reporter*, May 1, 1998.

———. 1998c. "In Tug of War at Synod, Curia Gets the Last Word." *National Catholic Reporter*, May 29, 1998.

———. 1998d. "Propositions Blend Asian, Roman View." *National Catholic Reporter*, May 29, 1998.

———. 1998e. "Report Faulted for Neglecting Asian Ideas." *National Catholic Reporter*, May 15, 1998.

———. 2002. *Pentecost in Asia: A New Way of Being Church.* Maryknoll, NY: Orbis.

General Secretariat of the Synod of Bishops. 1997. "'Lineamenta' for the Special Assembly of the Synod of Bishops for Asia." *Origins* 26 (31): 502–520.

Ghosh, Palash. 2013. "Virgin Mary in a Sari: Hindus Outraged by Christian Statue Depicting Blessed Mother and Jesus in Indian Tribal Dress." *International Business Times*, July 10, 2013. https://tinyurl.com/1ktma3rx.

Gillman, Ian Gillman, and Hans-Joachim Klimkeit. 1999. *Christians in Asia before 1500.* London: Routledge.

Goh, Cheng Teik. 1971. *The May Thirteenth Incident and Democracy in Malaysia.* Kuala Lumpur, Malaysia: Oxford University Press.

Gomes, Catherine, and Jonathan Y. Tan. 2015. "Christianity as a Culture of Mobility: A Case Study of Asian Transient Migrants in Singapore." *Kritika Kultura* 25:215–244.

———. 2017. "Christianity: A Culture of Mobility." In *Transient Mobility and Middle Class Identity: Media and Migration in Australia and Singapore*, by Catherine Gomes, 185–208. Singapore: Palgrave Macmillan.

Gómez, Felipe. 1986. "The Missionary Activity Twenty Years after Vatican II." *East Asian Pastoral Review* 23:26–57.

Gonsalves, Francis. 2008. "Carrying in Our Bodies the Marks of His Passion." *Vidyajyoti Journal of Theological Reflection* 72:801–807.

Gopal, Sarvepalli. 1993. *Anatomy of a Confrontation: The Rise of Communal Politics in India*. London: Zed.

Grant, Patrick. 2009. *Buddhism and Ethnic Conflict in Sri Lanka*. Albany, NY: SUNY.

Greenlee, David, ed. 2013. *Longing for Community: Church, Ummah, or Somewhere in Between?* Pasadena: William Carey Library.

Hayward, Susan. 2011. "The Spoiler and the Reconciler: Buddhism and the Peace Process in Sri Lanka." In *Between Terror and Tolerance: Religious Leaders, Conflict, and Peacemaking*, edited by Timothy D. Sisk, 183–200. Washington, DC: Georgetown University Press.

Hebblethwaite, Margaret. 1998a. "Dance of Joy Opens the Asian Synod in Rome." *Tablet*, April 25, 1998.

———. 1998b. "Opposing Lobbies United as Asian Synod Ends." *Tablet*, May 23, 1998.

———. 1998c. "Synod in Rome on Long Path to Enlightenment." *Tablet*, May 9, 1998.

Hoefer, Herbert E. 2001. *Churchless Christianity*. Pasadena: William Carey Library.

———. 2002. "Jesus, My Master: 'Jesu Bhakta' Hindu Christian Theology." *International Journal of Frontier Missions* 19 (3): 39–42.

Hogg, W. Richey. 1980. "Edinburgh 1910—Perspective 1980." *Occasional Bulletin of Missionary Research* 4 (4): 146–153.

Indonesian Catholic bishops. 1998. "Responses to the *Lineamenta*." *East Asian Pastoral Review* 35:54–85.

International Organization for Migration (IOM). 2011. *World Migration Report 2011*. Geneva: IOM.

Irvin, Dale T., and Scott W. Sunquist. 2001. *History of the World Christian Movement*. Vol. 1, *Earliest Christianity to 1453*. Maryknoll, NY: Orbis.

Janson, Marloes. 2016. "Unity through Diversity: A Case Study of Chrislam in Lagos." *Africa: Journal of the International African Institute* 86 (4): 646–672.

Japanese Catholic bishops. 1998. "Responses to the *Lineamenta*." *East Asian Pastoral Review* 35:86–111.

Jenkins, Philip. 2009. *The Lost History of Christianity: The Thousand-Year Golden Age of the Church in the Middle East, Africa and Asia and How It Died*. San Francisco: HarperOne.

John, Cyril. 2010. "Lay Movements and New Communities in the Life and Mission of the Church in Asia: Experiences from the Catholic Charismatic Renewal." Paper presented at the Congress of Asian Catholic Laity, Seoul, South Korea.

John, T. K. 1987. "The Pope's 'Pastoral Visit' to India: A Further Reflection." *Vidyajyoti Journal of Theological Reflection* 51:58–66.

John Paul II, Pope. 1994. "Tertio millennio adveniente." *Origins* 24:401–416.

———. 1996. "Message for World Migration Day on Undocumented Migrants." Vatican, July 25, 1995. https://tinyurl.com/kzvh5dbp.

———. 1999. "Religion and Peace Together." Address at the cathedral of Delhi. *Origins* 29 (1999): 399–400.

———. 2002. "Migration and Inter-religious Dialogue." Message of the Holy Father for the eighty-eighth World Day of Migration. Vatican, July 25, 2001. https://tinyurl.com/zcmjpzxc.

Jones, Owen Bennett. 2009. *Pakistan: Eye of the Storm.* 3rd ed. New Haven, CT: Yale University Press.

Kahn, Joel S., and Francis Loh Kok Wah, eds. 1992. *Fragmented Vision: Culture and Politics in Contemporary Malaysia.* Honolulu: University of Hawai'i Press.

Kavunkal, Jacob. 1995. "Asian Mission Theology." In *Towards an Asian Theology of Mission,* edited by Michael T. Seigel and Leonardo N. Mercado, 94–118. Manila: Divine Word.

Kuttiyanikkal, Ciril J. 2014. *Khrist Bhakta Movement: A Model for an Indian Church? Inculturation in the Area of Community Building.* Zurich: LIT.

Kwan, Simon Shui-Man. 2014. *Postcolonial Resistance and Asian Theology.* London: Routledge.

Lian Xi. 2010. *Redeemed by Fire: The Rise of Popular Christianity in Modern China.* New Haven, CT: Yale University Press.

Lie, John. 1995. "From International Migration to Transnational Diaspora." *Contemporary Sociology* 24 (4): 303–306.

Malaysia Department of Statistics. 2011. *Population Distribution and Basic Demographic Characteristic Report 2010.* July 29, 2011. https://tinyurl.com/53uohgpc.

Metropolitan Archdiocese of Kuala Lumpur. n.d. "About Archbishop Julian Leow." Metropolitan Archdiocese of Kuala Lumpur. Accessed February 17, 2021. https://tinyurl.com/482k9m28.

Moffett, Samuel Hugh. 1998. *A History of Christianity in Asia.* Vol. 1, *Beginnings to 1500.* 2nd rev. and corr. ed. Maryknoll, NY: Orbis.

Moreau, A. Scott. 2012. *Contextualization in World Mission: Mapping and Assessing Evangelical Models*. Grand Rapids, MI: Kregel.

Murad, Dina. 2014. "Father Julian Leow Is New Archbishop of Kuala Lumpur." *Star Online*, July 3, 2014. https://tinyurl.com/1ine4gam.

Neill, Stephen. 1984. *A History of Christianity in India: The Beginnings to AD 1707*. Cambridge: Cambridge University Press.

———. 1990. *A History of Christian Missions*. 2nd ed. Revised by Owen Chadwick. Harmondsworth, England: Penguin.

Pak, Jennifer. 2013. "The Man behind Malaysia's Interfaith Tours." BBC News, October 22, 2013. http://www.bbc.com/news/world-asia-24583935.

Parreñas, Rhacel Salazar. 2001. *Servants of Globalization: Women, Migration, and Domestic Work*. Stanford, CA: Stanford University Press.

Pechilis, Karen, and Selva J. Raj, eds. 2013. *South Asian Religions: Tradition and Today*. New York: Routledge.

Pew Research Center's Forum on Religion and Public Life. 2011. *Global Christianity: A Report on the Size and Distribution of the World's Christian Population*. Washington, DC: Pew Research Center.

Phan, Peter C. 2000. "*Ecclesia in Asia*: Challenges for Asian Christianity." *East Asian Pastoral Review* 37:215–232.

———. 2002. *The Asian Synod: Texts and Commentaries*. Maryknoll, NY: Orbis.

———. 2003a. *In Our Own Tongues: Perspectives from Asia on Mission and Inculturation*. Maryknoll, NY: Orbis.

———. 2003b. Review of *Introducing Theologies of Religion*, by Paul Knitter. *Horizons* 30:113–117.

———. 2018. *Asian Christianities: History, Theology, Practice*. Maryknoll, NY: Orbis.

Pieris, Aloysius. 1988. *An Asian Theology of Liberation*. Maryknoll, NY: Orbis.

Pontifical Council for the Pastoral Care of Migrants and Itinerant People. 2004. "Instruction: *Erga migrantes caritas Christi*." Vatican, 2004. https://tinyurl.com/4kf8wpz7.

Prior, John Mansford. 1998. "A Tale of Two Synods: Observations on the Special Assembly for Asia." *Vidyajyoti Journal of Theological Reflection* 62:654–665.

Quatra, Miguel Marcelo Quatra. 2000. *At the Side of the Multitudes: The Kingdom of God and the Mission of the Church in the FABC Documents (1970–1985)*. Quezon City, Philippines: Claretian.

Raj, Selva J., and Corinne G. Dempsey, eds. 2002. *Popular Christianity in India: Riting between the Lines*. Albany, NY: SUNY.

Rasiah, Jeyaraj. 2011. "Sri Lanka." In *Christianities in Asia*, edited by Peter C. Phan, 45–59. New York: Wiley-Blackwell.

Roberson, Ronald G. 2008. *The Eastern Christian Churches: A Brief Survey.* 7th rev. ed. Rome: Pontificio Istituto Orientale.

Rosales, Gaudencio B., and C. G. Arévalo, eds. 1992. *For All the Peoples of Asia: Federation of Asian Bishops' Conferences Documents from 1970–1991.* Maryknoll, NY: Orbis.

Said, Edward W. 1978. *Orientalism.* New York: Random House.

San Chirico, Kerry P. C. 2014. "Between Christian and Hindu: *Khrist Bhaktas,* Catholics and the Negotiation of Devotion in the Banaras Region." In *Constructing Indian Christianities: Culture, Conversion and Caste,* edited by Chad Bauman and Richard Fox Young, 23–44. New Delhi: Routledge.

Seager, Richard Hughes. 2006. *Encountering the Dharma: Daisaku Ikeda, Soka Gakkai, and the Globalization of Buddhist Humanism.* Berkeley: University of California Press.

Senanayake, Darini Rajasingham. 2009. *Buddhism and the Legitimation of Power: Democracy, Public Religion and Minorities in Sri Lanka.* Singapore: National University of Singapore Institute of South Asian Studies.

Sharma, Arvind, ed. 2001. *Hinduism and Secularism: After Ayodhya.* New York: Palgrave.

Shorter, Aylward. 1994. *Evangelization and Culture.* London: Geoffrey Chapman.

Stanley, Brian. 2009. *The World Missionary Conference, Edinburgh 1910.* Grand Rapids, MI: William B. Eerdmans.

Sugirtharajah, R. S. 2006. "Charting the Aftermath: A Review of Postcolonial Criticism." In *The Postcolonial Biblical Reader,* edited by R. S. Sugirtharajah, 7–32. Oxford: Blackwell.

Sylvester, Jerome G. 2013a. "The Khristbhakta Movement: A New Paradigm of Faith in Christ Jesus, Part I." *Vidyajyoti Journal of Theological Reflection* 27:345–359.

———. 2013b. "The Khristbhakta Movement: A New Paradigm of Faith in Christ Jesus, Part II." *Vidyajyoti Journal of Theological Reflection* 27:443–456.

———. 2013c. *Khristbhakta Movement: Hermeneutics of a Religio-cultural Phenomenon.* Delhi: ISPCK.

Tagle, Luis Antonio. 1998. "The Synod for Asia as Event." *East Asian Pastoral Review* 35:366–378.

Talman, Harley, and John Jay Travis. 2015. *Understanding Insider Movements: Disciples of Jesus within Diverse Religious Communities.* Pasadena: William Carey Library.

Tambiah, Stanley J. 1992. *Buddhism Betrayed? Religion, Politics and Violence in Sri Lanka*. Chicago: University of Chicago Press.

Tan, Jonathan Y. 2000. "Theologizing at the Service of Life: The Contextual Theological Methodology of the Federation of Asian Bishops' Conferences (FABC)." *Gregorianum* 81 (3): 541–575.

———. 2001. "Constructing an Asian Theology of Liturgical Inculturation from the Documents of the Federation of Asian Bishops' Conferences (FABC)." *Vidyajyoti Journal of Theological Reflection* 65:565–580.

———. 2002. "The Responses of the Indonesian and Japanese Bishops to the *Lineamenta*." In *The Asian Synod: Texts and Commentaries*, edited by Peter C. Phan, 59–72. Maryknoll, NY: Orbis.

———. 2003a. "Approaches to Christian Mission in Asia, I." *Vidyajyoti Journal of Theological Reflection* 67:214–230.

———. 2003b. "Approaches to Christian Mission in Asia, II." *Vidyajyoti Journal of Theological Reflection* 67:272–284.

———. 2004a. "From *Ecclesia in Asia* to *a Mission of Love and Service*: A Comparative Analysis of Two Contrasting Approaches to Doing Christian Mission in Asia." *East Asian Pastoral Review* 41 (1): 68–101.

———. 2004b. "From 'Missio *ad* Gentes' to 'Missio *inter* Gentes': Shaping a New Paradigm for Doing Christian Mission in Asia, Part 1." *Vidyajyoti Journal of Theological Reflection* 68:670–686.

———. 2004c. "*Missio inter Gentes*: Towards a New Paradigm in the Mission Theology of the Federation of Asian Bishops' Conferences." *Mission Studies* 21 (1): 65–95.

———. 2005a. "From 'Missio *ad* Gentes' to 'Missio *inter* Gentes': Shaping a New Paradigm for Doing Christian Mission in Asia, Part 2." *Vidyajyoti Journal of Theological Reflection* 69:27–41.

———. 2005b. "Missio inter Gentes." *Spiritus: Hors Serie 2005: Ad Gentes 40 ans après*: 147–157.

———. 2005c. "Missio inter Gentes: Vers uns nouveau paradigme de la theologie missionnaire." *Mission: Revue des sciences de la mission* 12 (1): 99–128.

———. 2005d. "A New Way of Being Church in Asia: The Federation of Asian Bishops' Conferences (FABC) at the Service of Life in Pluralistic Asia." *Missiology* 33 (1): 71–94.

———. 2006a. "La Chiesa e il Regno: Un nuovo modo essere Chiesa in Asia." In *Teologia in Asia*, edited by M. Amaladoss and R. Gibellini, 320–342. Brescia, Italy: Editrice Queriniana.

———. 2006b. *Menuju Suatu Paradigma Baru Dalam Teologi Misi*. Jakarta, Indonesia: Komisi Komunikasi Sosial Konferensi Waligereja Indonesia.

———. 2011. "Inculturation in Asia: The Asian Approach of the Federation of Asian Bishops' Conferences (FABC)." In *Reaping a Harvest from the Asian Soil: Towards an Asian Theology*, edited by Vimal Tirimanna, 81–100. Bangalore, India: Asian Trading Corporation.

———. 2012. "Migration in Asia and Its Missiological Implications: Insights from the Migration Theology of the Federation of Asian Bishops' Conferences (FABC)." *Mission Studies* 29:45–61.

———. 2013. "From 'Ad Gentes' to 'Active Integral Evangelization': The Reception of Vatican II's Mission Theology in Asia." *East Asian Pastoral Review* 50 (3): 217–250.

Tan, Paul Chee Ing, and Theresa Ee. 1984. Introduction to *Contemporary Issues on Malaysian Religions*, edited by Tunku Abdul Rahman Putra, Tan Sri Dr. Tan Chee Khoon, Dr. Chandra Muzaffar, and Lim Kit Siang, 5–16. Petaling Jaya, Malaysia: Pelanduk.

Teixeira, Manuel. 1963. *The Portuguese Missions in Malacca and Singapore (1511–1958)*. 3 vols. Lisbon: Agência-Geral do Ultramar.

Thangaraj, M. Thomas. 1999. *The Common Task: A Theology of Christian Mission*. Nashville: Abingdon.

Tirimanna, Vimal. 2014. *For All the Peoples of Asia*. Vol. 5, *Federation of Asian Bishops' Conferences Documents from 2007–2012*. Quezon City, Philippines: Claretian.

Union of Catholic Asian News (UCAN). 1998a. "Church Identity, Interreligious Dialogue, Justice among Synod Addresses." April 27, 1998. https://tinyurl.com/1t2p1gax.

———. 1998b. "Church Wishes to Work and Share Faith with All Asians, Synod Says." May 14, 1998. https://tinyurl.com/7g4icov3.

———. 1998c. "Pope John Paul Closes Synod for Asia with Solemn Mass and Farewell Lunch." May 18, 1998. https://tinyurl.com/4zyqfyqc.

———. 1998d. "Pope Names Special Members, Experts, Observers for Synod for Asia." April 9, 1998. https://tinyurl.com/3mde9tmn.

———. 1998e. "Presidents, Relator, Secretary Appointed for Synod for Asia." February 27, 1998. https://tinyurl.com/76vmfbkb.

———. 1998f. "Relations with Islam, Role of Family and Youth Will Impact Church, Synod Told." April 29, 1998. https://tinyurl.com/vfytu720.

———. 1998g. "Synod Asked to Affirm Asian Way of Evangelizing in a Decentralized Church." May 7, 1998. https://tinyurl.com/17mynw5u.

Vatican. 1990. *Codex Canonum Ecclesiarum Orientalium (CCEO)*. Rome: Libreria Editrice Vaticana. https://tinyurl.com/dpvj9c7y. English translation: https://tinyurl.com/jajjee9k.

Walbridge, Linda. 2002. *Christians of Pakistan: The Passion of Bishop John Joseph*. New York: Routledge.

Walters, Albert Sundararaj. 2002. *We Believe in One God? Reflections on the Trinity in the Malaysian Context*. Delhi: ISPCK.

———. 2007. "Issues in Christian-Muslim Relations: A Malaysian Christian Perspective." *Islam and Christian-Muslim Relations* 18 (1): 67–83.

Wetchgama, Banpote. 2014. "The New Buddhists: How Buddhists Can Follow Christ." *Mission Frontiers* 36 (6): 28–31.

Wiegele, Katharine L. 2005. *Investing in Miracles: El Shaddai and the Transformation of Popular Catholicism in the Philippines*. Honolulu: University of Hawai'i Press.

Wiest, Jean-Paul. 2007. "Chinese Youth and Religion Today." *Origins* 36 (33): 527–531.

Wilfred, Felix. 1988. "Inculturation as a Hermeneutical Question." *Vidyajyoti* 52:422–436.

———. 1990. "Fifth Plenary Assembly of FABC: An Interpretation of its Theological Orientation." *Vidyajyoti Journal of Theological Reflection* 54:583–592.

———. 1992. "The Federation of Asian Bishops' Conferences (FABC): Orientations, Challenges and Impact." In *For All the Peoples of Asia: Federation of Asian Bishops' Conferences Documents from 1970–1991*, edited by Gaudencio B. Rosales and C. G. Arévalo, xxiii–xxx. Maryknoll, NY: Orbis.

———. 1998. "What the Spirit Says to the Churches (Rev 2:7) A Vademecum on the Pastoral and Theological Orientations of the Federation of Asian Bishops' Conferences (FABC)." *Vidyajyoti* 62:124–133.

Williams, Corey L. 2019. "Chrislam, Accommodation and the Politics of Religious *Bricolage* in Nigeria." *Studies in World Christianity* 25 (1): 5–28.

Williams, Rowan. 2007. "Christianity in the Reinvention of China." *China Review* 40:1–3.

World Bank. 2011. *Migration and Remittances Factbook, 2011*. Washington, DC: World Bank.

World Council of Churches. 2004. *Ecumenical Considerations for Dialogue and Relations with People of Other Religions*. Geneva: World Council of Churches.

Yango, Emo. 2016. "A Christology from below in Muslim Magindanon Context." In *Christologies, Cultures, and Religions: Portraits of Christ in the Philippines*, edited by Pascal D. Bazzell and Aldrin Peñamora, chap. 9. Mandaluyong City, Philippines: OMF Literature. Kindle.

Young, Ernest P. 2013. *Ecclesiastical Colony: China's Catholic Church and the French Religious Protectorate*. New York: Oxford University Press.

Index